Progressive Policies for Economic Development

Despite the unprecedented gravity of the challenges posed by global warming, most political systems have not given them the required priority. The oil industry has resisted, and many countries have taken only token measures to reduce emissions and mitigate the worst effects. In this context, this book examines the progressive options available to today's developing countries as they face the limitations of neoliberalism and the existential challenge of global warming.

Examining the cases of both low-income fossil-fuel-dependent economies and large middle-income economies, this book argues that for all developing economies the best way forward includes "green" macroeconomic policies articulated with progressive industrial and social policies, because they will allow these countries to achieve economic diversification, build alternative drivers of growth, and deliver improvements in the distribution of income, wealth, and power. There is urgent need for this progressive policy agenda—grounded in heterodox economics and committed to social integration and the reduction of multiple inequalities—to improve the economic outcomes for these countries, improve the lives of their citizens, and help them meet their global climate targets. The book argues that capitalism challenges the possibility of free and dignified existence while climate change challenges the possibility of life itself, and that the challenges that the former and the latter pose must be confronted together. Since neoliberal capitalism will not adopt the necessary policies to reduce carbon emissions rapidly, it must be overthrown—not only for ethical or logical reasons, or to shift to better arrangements for the functioning of society, but also in order to preserve the conditions necessary for life itself.

This agenda for progressive economic development is essential reading for anyone interested in heterodox economics, development studies, international politics, international relations, or sustainable business.

Alfredo Saad-Filho is Professor of Political Economy and International Development at King's College London, UK.

Progressive Policies for Economic Development

Economic Diversification and Social
Inclusion after Climate Change

Alfredo Saad-Filho

Routledge
Taylor & Francis Group

LONDON AND NEW YORK

First published 2022
by Routledge
2 Park Square, Milton Park, Abingdon, Oxon OX14 4RN

and by Routledge
605 Third Avenue, New York, NY 10158

Routledge is an imprint of the Taylor & Francis Group, an informa business

British Library Cataloguing-in-Publication Data
A catalogue record for this book is available from the British Library

Library of Congress Cataloging-in-Publication Data
A catalog record has been requested for this book

ISBN: 978-0-367-61044-9 (hbk)
ISBN: 978-0-367-61045-6 (pbk)
ISBN: 978-1-003-10303-5 (ebk)

Typeset in Times New Roman
by Taylor & Francis Books

Contents

Acknowledgements

This book builds upon a report commissioned by Oxfam America, 'Climate Change and Oil-Dependent Countries: An Agenda for Economic Diversification and Social Inclusion'. I am grateful to James Morrissey for his support during the preparation of that report.

Abbreviations

AAUs:	Assigned amount units
AEs:	Advanced capitalist economies
CBDR:	Common but differentiated responsibilities
CGD:	Commission for Growth and Development
CO2e:	CO2 equivalent
DECS:	Democratic economic strategy
DEPs:	Democratic economic policies
DEs:	Developing economies
GFC:	Global Financial Crisis
IFIs:	International financial institutions
IMF:	International Monetary Fund
IPCC:	Intergovernmental Panel on Climate Change
MDGs:	Millennium development goals
NGOs:	Non-Governmental Organisations
NICs:	Newly Industrialising Economies
NIE:	New Institutional Economics
ODA:	Overseas development assistance
PPD:	Pro-poor development
PWC:	Post-Washington Consensus
(P)WC:	Washington Consensus and post-Washington Consensus
R2D:	Right to development
SDGs:	Sustainable development goals
UK:	United Kingdom
UNFCCC:	United Nations Framework Convention on Climate Change
US, USA:	United States of America
WC:	Washington Consensus
WEO:	World Environmental Organisation

Introduction

This book is about economic policy alternatives to neoliberalism in the context of rapid climate change and a global environmental crisis. I have examined neoliberalism in several written works and have advocated for progressive, democratic, and distributive economic policy options for many years.[1] This critical engagement with contemporary capitalism can be extended to the environmental constraint and the impending climate disaster: in order to build a democratic economy and a substantively (and not merely formally) free society, we must, first of all, be *alive*. This is not about the troubles of a small number of privileged souls who can fund well-protected shelters for themselves and their families; it is about averting disaster for billions of people whose homes will be flooded, or whose lands will become parched, or whose sources of income will disappear, and it is about defending entire regions and even whole countries that may disappear beneath the waves because of a catastrophe that can be limited but no longer avoided entirely.

Humans and our sister species have confronted few greater challenges in their time on Earth. It may be that disaster has become unavoidable, and that a succession of environmental calamities are certain to afflict us: devastating forest fires, unprecedentedly strong and frequent hurricanes, scorching heat, rising seawaters that will swallow up homes, roads, farms, lives, and livelihoods, and so on. This is not just about the weather: *capitalism kills*. For decades, we have known that the unbridled drive to accumulate turns most humans into servants of infinitely greedy masters, who live in luxury through extractions from their fellows—they always want more. We have also discovered that, in seeking to produce infinite quantities of value to enrich those who are already privileged, capitalism also squanders staggering amounts of wealth. This mode of production extracts resources wherever they can be found, and destroys the planet as it seeks to convert materials and the powers of nature into profits. *The most important claim in this book*

*is that the challenge of capitalism against a free and dignified existence
and the challenge of climate change against life itself must be confronted
together.* These challenges cannot be addressed separately, for example,
by "everyone, rich and poor, in all countries" first coming together
around a progressive-capitalist-green-growth program to save the planet
and then, only when that has been accomplished, starting to push against
the "green capitalist" state, gradually bending the boundaries of the possible until they can burst through the gates of the White House, Kremlin,
Elysée, Downing Street, and so on, in order to create a revolutionary eco-
socialist society. This scenario is sadly impractical and wholly unrealistic.

Political change and the transformation of our energy matrix must
be pursued together, and immediately. Since neoliberal capitalism will
not adopt the policies needed to reduce carbon emissions rapidly, it
must be overthrown. It must be defeated for other reasons too: its
abusive patterns of employment; obscene rates of exploitation; perverse
modes of distribution; obsession with pointless consumption; over-
production of financial assets; accumulation of unpayable debts;
degradation of democracy; unprecedented corruption; mounting dis-
equilibria; and injustices at every juncture. There is a sense in which
the environmental crisis merely adds another item to the list of unacceptable features of capitalism; but this item is both urgent and overwhelming, since it concerns not only ethical, logical, or preferential
arrangements for the good functioning of society, but the conditions
for its very existence.

This book, then, is about challenging neoliberalism understood as
the contemporary form, phase, or mode of existence of capitalism. The
book is not primarily about changes in the climate, or about necessary,
past, or ongoing mobilizations to change the world. The book touches
on them, but it focuses on the disproportionate burden of climate
change upon the poor and the world's poor countries, and the need to
shift the cost of the coming disasters away from the most vulnerable
and toward those with the broadest shoulders, greatest resources, and a
track record of gains from the inequities imposed by capitalism and
reproduced by neoliberalism. In doing this, the analysis stresses the
crises and policy dilemmas in the developing economies (DEs), which
are bound to confront the toughest challenges because of their comparative lack of resources, technologies, efficient institutions, and social
cohesion vis-à-vis the advanced capitalist economies (AEs). This book
outlines the potential implications of climate change for the economy,
politics, and society, and it sketches a set of progressive economic
policy alternatives to address the twin challenges of climate change
(which refers to capitalism as a mode of production) and inequality

(which, in its current form, refers to neoliberalism). The book shows that the majority of the population in most countries can benefit from integrated policies to promote structural economic changes for environmental sustainability,[2] improve the distribution of income, wealth, and assets, and expand political and economic democracy. It is a key claim of this book that the struggles to achieve these latter three objectives are essential, equally urgent and mutually reinforcing.

Why change anything?

There is overwhelming evidence that the Earth's climate is warming up, and that global warming has been accelerating (IPCC Working Group I 1995, 2018; UNFCCC 2018a). Human emissions of CO_2e (CO_2 equivalent) gases have already raised temperatures by at least 1 degree Celsius from the pre–Industrial Revolution baseline, and current trends suggest that temperatures could rise by up to seven degrees in the next 100 years (Baer 2012; Granados 2018; McKibben 2011b).[3] Anything approaching this outcome would be incompatible with life as we know it. Global warming is already having severe consequences:

> The Arctic has lost twenty-five percent of its summer ice cover, and the melt on Greenland is proceeding with unnerving speed … The hydrological cycle is fundamentally disrupted, with both more droughts and far more extreme rainfall events … The oceans have become steadily more acidic … Forest fires are raging with newfound intensity, and forests in the boreal regions are dying from onslaughts of insects once kept in check by cold winter temperatures … Crop yields have become erratic, with serious busts as heat waves wipe out whole growing regions … Mosquito-borne diseases … have spread rapidly … Political tensions have begun to flare over water shortages and refugee fears … [and] [s]mall, low-lying islands have been evacuated as rising seas have made habitation impossible.
>
> (McKibben 2011b; see also Granados 2018 and ODI 2013).

Unquestionably, the heaviest impact of climate change will be felt by the poor countries and the poor everywhere, by virtue of their vulnerability to *any* economic disturbance. This includes, but is not limited to, "325 million extremely poor people … living in the 49 most hazard-prone countries in 2030, the majority in South Asia and sub-Saharan Africa" (ODI 2013).

Delays reducing global emissions will make it harder to confront these challenges. Specifically, the costs of mitigation tend to increase exponentially, since impacts worsen and cheaper options disappear as economies gradually lock themselves into high carbon infrastructures, systems of production, and patterns of consumption. This implies that it would be impossible to "compensate" slow progress in mitigation today through faster progress in the future. Instead, delays in emissions cuts will impose increasingly steep reduction curves, potentially to the point where reasonable targets for global warming become unachievable for technological or political reasons. Even worse, the inertia of the climate system implies that overshooting greenhouse gas emissions in the coming decades could compromise temperatures for millennia (WDR 2010).

Despite the unprecedented gravity of these challenges, most political systems have not given them the required priority, the oil industry (probably the most powerful lobby in the world) has predictably resisted, and many countries have taken only token measures to reduce emissions and mitigate global warming. These policies of inaction, at least while profits can be captured by means of the dominant energy and production matrices, have been blessed by mainstream (conventional, orthodox, or neoclassical) economics. The dominant modality of economics focuses on the static maximization of profits and consumer "utility" with given resources, which tilts the analysis toward short-termism and the avoidance of costly and uncertain structural economic transformations. Inevitably, mainstream economics validates unsustainable levels of extraction of fossil fuels and other resources,[4] predatory modes of production, wasteful consumption, and the concentration of income, wealth, and power.[5]

Attempts to address these challenges piecemeal are bound to fail. On the one hand, it is impossible to reduce our dependence on fossil fuels gradually within the distributional framework imposed by global neoliberalism. This is because the dominant interests are locked into a logic of overconsumption by the privileged and short-termist financialized profit extraction that is incompatible with high-cost, long-term investment to change the pattern of economic reproduction. Neoliberalism and financialization will delay and downgrade all attempts to address climate change until it becomes too late; in doing so, they will drive the world into the abyss of environmental collapse and mass extinction.[6] On the other hand, attempts to rebalance the global economy and redistribute income between and within nations while ignoring the environmental challenge will also drive the world over the edge. The message is that it is *impossible* to produce more, consume more, and equalize living standards upward using existing technologies and those that can be developed in the time available under neoliberalism.

The rhythm of climate change implies that humans will not be in the world long enough to enjoy a more prosperous and more equal future, *unless* it is delivered together with, and through, a new system of accumulation.

This book examines the progressive policy options available today, focusing primarily on the DEs as they face the twin challenges of global warming and neoliberalism. The difficulties confronting two sets of developing countries are examined in greater detail. First are the low-income fossil-fuel-dependent economies: since CO2e emissions must decline rapidly, global oil markets will either contract in an orderly way through coordinated cuts in supply and demand, or they will crash when economies eventually stampede away from oil, or when climate disasters finally overwhelm the interests committed to "business as usual" (Gaulin and Le Billon 2020). Second are the large middle-income economies, which have already achieved some degree of diversification and manufacturing growth, and which have much greater potential than the poorest countries to implement progressive economic policies.[7] In both cases, the best way to diversify the economy, build alternative drivers of growth, and improve the distribution of income, wealth, and power is through a combination of "green" industrial policies with democratic macroeconomic and social policies. This progressive agenda is urgently needed for four specific reasons.

First, there is *the global carbon budget*. The carbon budget links global emissions with a given temperature limit. The calculation is sobering: the potential emissions from the oil and gas fields and coal mines already in operation would warm the planet beyond two degrees; the potential emissions from the already-existing oil and gas fields alone would take the world beyond one-and-a-half degrees (Hansen et al. 2008; McKinnon et al. 2017).[8] In order to preserve recognizable forms of life on Earth, countries *must not* consume all the fossil fuels that are technically recoverable; consequently, much of the known reserves of oil can *never* be extracted, and *no further prospection* should take place (SEI, IISD, ODI, E3G, and UNEP 2020; these calculations are subject to changes in distribution, since the rich consume much more than the poor; see Kartha et al. 2020).

Second, there is *the imperative of diversification*. It follows from the previous point that oil-producing economies *must* diversify away from fossil fuels as rapidly as possible (Bendell 2018; Lahn and Bradley 2016). Scholars and policymakers have long recognized that excessive dependence on the production and export of primary commodities (i.e., unprocessed mineral and agricultural products) is potentially problematic, especially for DEs. Potential disadvantages include the risk of building economic enclaves with limited production, employment, technological, and other linkages with the wider economy; the tendency toward the concentration of income, wealth, and power; vulnerability to external competition and declining terms of trade; and the likelihood of technological, demand, price, and other structural shifts in the main markets. Several countries in the Global South must confront the challenge of diversification. Some are large (Russia, Saudi Arabia); others are small (Gabon, South Sudan); some have already achieved considerable diversification (Mexico, Qatar), while others remain heavily concentrated (Nigeria, Venezuela). Policies will be different in each case, and they will have to be applied sensitively in order to promote social cohesion, secure macroeconomic stability, and maximize the probability of success. Yet, firm action will be needed in every case. The oil-dependent AEs (Norway, Canada) will also face difficult challenges, but the stakes are lower because these economies are more productive, diversified, and resilient, and they have incomparably greater resources to address climate change.

Third, there is *the adverse distributional implications of neoliberalism.* The global transition to neoliberalism, which started in the mid-1970s, has led to regressive outcomes in terms of the distribution of income, wealth, and power in most countries (Alvaredo et al. 2018; Cornia and Martorano 2012; UNCTAD 2012); the only regional exception is Latin America during the "Pink Tide" in the mid-2000s. Neoliberalism has also been accompanied by the financialization of economic and social reproduction and the tendential decline of GDP growth rates almost everywhere. Neoliberalism and financialization lost legitimacy after the Global Financial Crisis (GFC) starting in 2007, and there is an urgent need for progressive and democratic policy alternatives. These pressures are likely to intensify as the global economy emerges from the stresses of the COVID-19 pandemic, which struck in 2020.

Fourth, there is *the potential to drive change.* The poorest countries are the most vulnerable to any disruption and need change most urgently, but they can least afford to address it. Middle-income countries are the most dynamic centers in the world economy, and, although they do not currently emit the most CO2e (this questionable distinction belongs to the AEs in the Global North), their emissions are growing rapidly. Yet, middle countries have got the resources and capabilities to lead by example, transform the global economy, and press the North to follow suit. Finally, the AEs have got resources and should have the motivation to change—but these economies are also less vulnerable to climate change and their elites, corporations, and governments benefit the most from the *status quo.*

How to change everything?

The goal of wholesale decarbonization (i.e., zero or negative human carbon footprint) highlights three *excessive concentrations* in the world economy: the global energy matrix is excessively concentrated around fossil fuels; the economic structure in several countries is excessively concentrated around oil, gas, and coal; and income, wealth, and power have become excessively concentrated under neoliberalism. The patterns of production and consumption built around these concentrated structures are similarly distorted: for example, production is too carbon-intensive and too biased toward the rich and the rich countries, which tend to over-consume and generate too much waste. (For a detailed study, see Kartha et al. 2020; their report shows that the world's richest 10% are responsible for 50% of emissions, while the poorest 50% are responsible for only 7%; worse still, emissions growth is heavily skewed toward the top of the world distribution of income.) Change is needed at all these levels. In particular, the global energy matrix must shift toward renewables; fossil fuels must be left in the ground; and the oil-export-dependent economies must diversify (Millward-Hopkins et al. 2020).

This book argues that these difficulties have not been confronted seriously by mainstream economists and neoliberal governments, and that they are unlikely to do so in the time available. For reasons of practicality, effectiveness, legitimacy, and sustainability, the necessary policy goals can be achieved only through the reversal of the income-concentrating logic of neoliberalism. In turn, progress will be constrained by the availability of financing and the need for macro-economic stability. This book argues that solutions must be found at the global *and* national levels simultaneously. It will be difficult to deliver these policy goals; however, inaction through hesitation, delays, or attempts to shift responsibility to others while continuing to reap short-term profits is unconscionable. *Every country, organization, business, and household must address climate change as an unprecedented challenge to life itself.* This is an existential task; failure to complete it will imply the extinction of countless species, possibly including our own. The stakes could not be higher.[9]

This book outlines a bold approach to address these challenges, focusing on a democratic economic strategy based on diversification (shifting the energy matrix and building resilience) *and* redistribution (promoting equality and building economic democracy). In this book, "economic diversification" concerns the rapid expansion of the non-oil sector in order to achieve a sustainable energy base and a more balanced distribution of economic activity in terms of output, exports, employment, and taxation. A "democratic" or "progressive" approach (these terms are treated as synonymous) is grounded on heterodox political economy, and it is committed to economic and political democracy, social integration, and the reduction of inequalities. This is not about one-off or marginal policy changes; it concerns the transformation of the dominant modes of production, exchange, consumption, and international integration, and the emergence of new social relations and a new type of human metabolism with nature.

Closing the feedback loop between mitigation, diversification, equality, and democratic governance can both drive *and* legitimize economic strategies to protect the environment and increase resilience and sustainability, benefiting the majority of people in most countries. This is the core of the democratic economic strategy (DECS) and the democratic economic policies (DEPs) outlined in this book. DECS and DEPs respond to the imperatives of equity, inclusion, democracy, diversification, sustainability, and social justice. They include policies to drive sustainable growth, promote the manufacturing sector, create employment, foster social inclusion and the satisfaction of basic needs, and improve the distribution of income, wealth, and power. These drivers of change are mutually reinforcing, and they can support the ambition to build a society inspired by progressive values rather than by environmentally destructive acquisitiveness.

The scale and complexity of these tasks raise the issue of the costs of transition. The basic principle is that the burden must be borne primarily by the rich and the AEs, since they have greater capacities, benefited the most from the destruction of the natural environment, and their patterns of production and consumption are disproportionately more carbon-intensive than those of the poor and the poorer countries. Decisive action will be needed both through country-level initiatives and through multilateral cooperation embedded in treaties with much greater scope and ambition than those achieved so far.

Mainstream economics is unprepared to address these challenges. This approach to economics ignores almost entirely the need to reduce greenhouse gas emissions drastically and urgently. It lacks the tools to comprehend the challenge, and cannot devise policies to address it in the short term. Instead, it offers faith-based claims that the "correct" prices emerging from (non-existent) "perfect" markets would allocate losses smoothly and fairly and create the "right" incentives, and that technological fixes will become available before runaway climate change destroys recognizable modes of life. This is both misguided and wholly insufficient, given the task at hand.

The book

This book includes this introduction, seven substantive chapters, and a conclusion. The first chapter offers a political economy review of the drivers, impact, and severity of climate change; the reasons why the latter has not been addressed decisively under neoliberalism; and the role of financialization. The second addresses the imperatives to engage with climate change, and the principles to do so, in the Global North and in the Global South. This includes the need to leave oil in the ground and the way to distribute the costs through the principle of common but differentiated responsibilities (CBDR). The third reviews the most influential debates around economic concentration and diversification. It focuses on the contrast between neoclassical approaches, which stress the gains from trade due to specialization, and heterodox views arguing that diversification in general and the expansion of the manufacturing sector in particular are essential for rapid, sustained, and stable economic growth. These debates were complicated in recent decades by the identification by the mainstream (i.e., mainstream economists) of a "resource curse" and "Dutch disease," which could lend support to diversification; in turn, the (heterodox and sometimes radical) Latin American "Pink Tide" administrations have confounded their supporters by remaining attached to primary production and resource extraction, instead of pushing for economic diversification and manufacturing sector growth. The fourth outlines the principles of progressive development strategies, including the need to transcend neoliberalism and financialization in order to build a democratic economy and society. Democratic economic strategies can be related to five key areas of debate in the field of international development: (a) poverty;(b) distribution; (c) the environment; (d) policy instruments and goals (including fiscal monetary and financial policies, the role of public investment, the balance of payments constraint, social policies, and equity); and (e) democracy and the protection of identities. The fifth examines the arguments for and against economic growth, and the role of growth in a democratic economic strategy. The sixth reviews in detail the policy options to address growth, diversification, distribution, and mitigation of climate change, drawing upon the heterodox literatures on industrial policy and on the literatures on pro-poor economic growth. Finally, the seventh focuses on the financing mechanisms that can underpin this democratic economic strategy.

This book is limited in several ways; the most significant of which is the impossibility of doing more than sketching the issues at stake and outlining possible solutions: this must be done in further studies. The book also does not consider individual country cases in detail, and does not differentiate the impact of climate change according to location, ethnicity, or gender. Despite these shortcomings, this book will achieve its goals if the democratic policy options outlined herein can help to foster debates about the best way forward for the majority of countries and the poorest peoples on Earth.

Notes

1 The concept of neoliberalism is examined in a vast literature. My own views (including references to alternative interpretations) are outlined in Fine and Saad-Filho (2017), Saad-Filho (2017, 2019, 2021), and Saad-Filho and Johnston (2005).
2 A general definition of sustainability is: "A level of ecological replenishment necessary not only for human futurity but for the continued existence of other species and their ecosystems" (Langley and Mellor 2002, p. 1; see also Yülek 2018).
3 Temperatures are given in Celsius unless otherwise specified.
4 "Fossil fuels," including oil, gas, and coal, or, for brevity, "oil," serve as shorthand for all primary resources that cannot be produced, processed, extracted or traded at will or until stocks are exhausted because of global imperatives; other examples include palm oil, because of deforestation; meat, for its imprint on the environment; and hard minerals (e.g., copper, iron, nickel, tin, lead, lithium, cobalt, gold, silver, and rare earth elements), for ecological reasons.
5 "The world and its societies are currently facing a triple crisis: ecologically, economically, and socially. The aim of ecological macroeconomics is to inform how these crises are interconnected, which crisis phenomena reduce to the same root cause, and how sustainable and equitable crisis responses could be formulated. The crises, however, are associated with particular socio-economic structures and practices and their solutions necessarily entail moral judgements which are beyond the limits of conventional macroeconomics" (Rezai and Stagl 2016, p. 184).
6 "In our political system … extraordinary profitability allows … energy companies an almost infinite ability to wield influence, especially when all they must do to win is delay action" (McKibben 2011b, p. 11).
7 This book treats the terms "low income," "poor," and "developing" countries as synonyms. These countries are disaggregated, when necessary, into "very poor" and "middle-income" countries. Similarly, "rich" and "advanced" economies are also treated as synonymous.
8 "Terrestrial ecosystems hold about 2,300 Gt of carbon – roughly 500 Gt in above-ground biomass and about three times that amount in the soils … The atmosphere currently contains about 824 gigatons (Gt) of carbon. Human-caused emissions of carbon in 2007 totaled about 9 Gt of carbon, of which about 7.7 Gt were from the combustion of fossil fuel and the rest were from changes in land cover … The atmospheric concentration of CO_2 is currently increasing at a rate of about 2 parts per million (ppm) a year,

which is equivalent to an increase in the atmospheric loading of carbon by about 4 Gt of carbon a year ... The rest of the CO_2 emissions are being taken up by "carbon sinks" – the ocean and terrestrial ecosystems. The oceans take up about 2 Gt of carbon a year ... It appears that terrestrial ecosystems are currently taking up the excess' (WDR 2010, p. 71; see also Baer 2012).

9 The need to confront global warming like a war is increasingly being recognized even in mainstream circles; see, for example, McKibben (2016).

1   Capitalism and the climate

Neoliberalism, as the current form, phase, or stage of capitalist production, is intrinsically exploitative of people and nature, and it is incompatible with the stability of the climate. Its logic of expanded accumulation driven by individual profit-making has led to rising CO2e emissions, the destruction of environments, and the elimination of countless species, and it has fatally destabilised the rhythms of nature. This chapter reviews the systemic roots of the changes in the Earth's climate and the drivers of the environmental damage caused by global capitalism. It also examines their political implications through, for example, the shocking inaction of even the most "sensible" democratic governments, given the magnitude of the unfolding disaster. Finally, the chapter outlines the case for curtailing rapidly the extraction of fossil fuels.

Capital accumulation, extraction, poverty

Capitalist production and the accumulation of capital rely on the employment of labor and the productive consumption of processed inputs and natural resources: minerals, agricultural products, and, especially, energy. There is no need to stress that the consumption of fossil fuels releases CO2 and other gases in such volumes that they are influencing the Earth's climate and triggering global warming. This has been known for decades, and these processes have been examined in multiple ways—for example, through the ecological implications of economic growth; the consequences of climate change for humans and other animals; the chemical, physical, geological and other processes involved; and the ethical and intergenerational costs and benefits of fossil fuels.[1] These debates invariably point to increasingly alarming scenarios. For example:

The eventual response to doubling pre-industrial atmospheric CO2 likely would be a nearly ice-free planet, preceded by a period of chaotic change with continually changing shorelines ... Humanity's task of moderating human-caused global climate change is urgent. Ocean and ice-sheet inertias provide a buffer delaying full response by centuries, but there is a danger that human-made forcings could drive the climate system beyond tipping points such that change proceeds out of our control.

(Hansen et al. 2008, p. 164)

In the meantime, large numbers of people already suffer from poverty and deprivation, which will become harder to address with climate change:

Climate change threatens all countries, with developing countries the most vulnerable. Estimates are that they would bear some 75 to 80 percent of the costs of damages caused by the changing climate. Even 2°C warming above preindustrial temperatures—the minimum the world is likely to experience—could result in permanent reductions in GDP of 4 to 5 percent for Africa and South Asia. Most developing countries lack sufficient financial and technical capacities to manage increasing climate risk. They also depend more directly on climate-sensitive natural resources for income and wellbeing. And most are in tropical and subtropical regions already subject to highly variable climate ... *Economic growth alone is unlikely to be fast or equitable enough to counter threats from climate change, particularly if it remains carbon intensive and accelerates global warming.*

(WDR 2010, p. xx)

Extraction, exploitation, exhaustion

Emissions of greenhouse gases change the climate in ways that are diffuse, gradual, cumulative, and global (Granados 2018). These relationships severely constrain the options available to limit climate change and mitigate its impact:

The climate system exhibits substantial inertia ... CO2 remains in the atmosphere for decades to centuries, so a decline in emissions takes time to affect concentrations. Temperatures lag concentrations: temperatures will continue increasing for a few centuries after concentrations have stabilized. And sea levels lag temperature reductions: the thermal expansion of the ocean from an increase in temperature will last 1,000 years or more while the sea-level rise from melting ice could last several millennia.

(WDR 2010, pp. 10–11)

The consequences are startling:

The dynamics of the climate system ... limit[s] how much future mitigation can be substituted for efforts today. For example, stabilizing the climate near 2°C (around 450 ppm of CO2e) would require global emissions to begin declining immediately by about 1.5 percent a year. A five-year delay would have to be offset by faster emission declines ... [A] ten-year delay in mitigation would most likely make it impossible to keep warming from exceeding 2°C ... Inertia is also a factor in research and development (R&D) and in the deployment of new technologies. New energy sources have historically taken about 50 years to reach half their potential. Substantial investments in R&D are needed now to ensure that new technologies are available and rapidly penetrating the marketplace in the near future. Innovation is also needed in transport, building, water management, urban design, and many other sectors that affect climate change and are in turn affected by climate change.

(WDR 2010, pp. 10–11)[2]

In other words, *time is not on our side.* Current environmental challenges are closely related to four sources of stress in the global economy.

First, and at the most general level, there is an irresolvable contradiction between the boundless search for individual profits under neoliberal capitalism, through extraction, production, exchange, speculation, and plunder, and the social consequences of the activities generating those profits, especially those flowing from the limited capacity of the Earth to sustain a stable climate. This is not simply a "technical" matter of absorptive capacity or carbon budgets. The underlying problem is that profitability requires the consumption of natural resources, but nature can never be fully commodified. The atmosphere, rivers, oceans, seasons, and the metabolic processes that produce what, for humans, appear as the "natural conditions of production," either have not (yet) been appropriated by capital, or cannot be claimed as property in any meaningful sense. The consequence is that they cannot be traded for profit in stable markets, and will *always* tend to be overexploited. By the same token, the boundary between "sustainable" and "unsustainable" plunder will *always* remain fuzzy, and nature will *always* tend to be used as a free sink for carbon and other wastes generated by the production of commodities for profitable sale.

Even when governments ascribe property rights over nature, or set arbitrary ("shadow" or any other) prices to natural processes, or impose specific taxes, charges, or subsidies, or create markets where property titles over resources and the environment can be traded, those institutions will affect economic outcomes only imperfectly and insufficiently from the point of view of the efforts needed to address climate change (Heynen et al. 2007; Siebert 2020). The difficulty is not merely that national governments are not "strong enough" to impose the "right" prices, taxes, charges, and subsidies in order to curtail extraction or shift demand enough to avoid environmental collapse; it is not even the (closely related) laxity of the existing international treaties. The trouble is that the necessary outcomes *cannot* be achieved by market processes. The inevitable consequences follow; for example, "the coal-fired power plants proposed around the world over the next 25 years are so numerous that their lifetime CO2 emissions would equal those of all coal-burning activities since the beginning of the industrial era" (WDR 2010, p. 11).

Second, there is a disjunction between the longstanding awareness of the environmental limits to growth and the evident inability of governments and intergovernmental organizations to do much to address climate change. More than a quarter-century since the United Nations Framework Convention on Climate Change (UNFCCC) came into force, little has been tried and even less has been achieved;[3] all signs point to catastrophic climate change within a couple of generations, with consequences likely to last for millennia. For an illustration of the limitations of current approaches, take the example of oil-export-dependent Norway, one of the wealthiest countries on Earth:

> Norway's emissions trajectory with proposed and prospective new oil and gas fields is not in line with the rate of global emissions reduction needed to achieve the Paris goals … [I]f Norway continues to permit exploration and development of new fields, it will both push the world into dangerous levels of climate change and risk billions of dollars of investment and thousands of jobs, forcing on itself (and others) a rapid transition at huge economic and social cost. Since carbon budgets are finite, Norway is set to take an undue share of limited global carbon budgets, thereby depriving poor countries of an opportunity to develop.
>
> (McKinnon et al. 2017, p. 2)

For similar reasons, CO2 emissions from oil, gas, and coal have risen almost relentlessly, from 20,516 megatons in 1990 to 33,513 megatons in 2018, declining temporarily only after the GFC (and, later, the COVID-19 pandemic).[4] Perversely, the share of the dirtiest fuel, coal, rose steadily between 1999 and 2014.[5]

The emissions of a small number of AEs have declined in recent years,[6] but these outcomes, especially in the United States and the United Kingdom, are largely due to deindustrialization and the relocation of "their" manufacturing output (and emissions) to the Global South. It would be misleading for the AEs to claim credit for these CO2 reductions, because they are by definition transfers that do not reflect improvements in technologies, do not challenge current living standards, and do nothing to address the climate disaster. Alarmingly, even if the CO2 reductions in the best-performing countries (Cuba, Denmark, Spain, and Sweden) were replicated everywhere, the world would *still* not achieve the targets set in the Paris agreement (Anderson et al. 2020; Granados 2018; Muttitt 2018). Take the example of Denmark:

> Denmark is a leader in technological innovation and wind power. A large fraction of the total energy consumed in that country is now produced by zero-emissions renewable sources. However ... the CO2 emissions implied by what is consumed in Denmark have not declined. Total energy consumption in Denmark in kilowatt-hours (kWh) slightly decreased from 228 billion kWh in 1990 to 210 billion kWh in 2014, while total production of renewable energy more than quadrupled from 13.3 to 54.5 billion kWh. But emissions of CO2 implied by total consumption in Denmark were 58 megatons in 1990, 55 megatons in 2014, and 54 megatons in 2015.
>
> (Granados 2018, p. 25)

Boyce comments on the lack of sufficient progress curbing carbon emissions, stating that:

> The 1997 Kyoto Protocol sought to cap the carbon dioxide emissions of industrialized countries at roughly 94% of their 1990 levels—a modest target ... In March 2001 the U.S. administration of President George W. Bush rejected this accord ... because it would impose costs on the U.S. economy while not setting emissions ceilings for developing countries.
>
> (Boyce 2004, p. 19)

Years later, President Donald Trump would take the United States out of the Paris agreement, stating that:

> The Paris accord would have been shutting down American producers with excessive regulatory restrictions like you would not believe, while allowing foreign producers to pollute with impunity ... What we won't do is punish the American people while enriching foreign polluters ... I'm proud to say it—it's called America First.[7]

These quotes neatly encapsulate the predicament of climate policy since the early 1990s: growing consensus in scientific circles, grudging recognition in political discourse, reluctant public policies, and recurrent backsliding by most political leaders.

Third, there is the contradiction between the accumulated emissions by the leading Western economies, on which basis they grew in the past, and the rapidly rising emissions in DEs. Understandably, the DEs claim the right to development (R2D) today, that is, with existing technologies, and argue that the remaining carbon budget should be made available primarily to the DEs rather than the AEs, since there is a strong relationship between emissions growth and poverty reduction (see Chapter 2):

> [R]egions that have seen extreme reductions in poverty, specifically East Asia and the Pacific and South Asia, have increased their carbon emissions by almost 200%. The only region that has decreased its carbon emissions over this time period, sub-Saharan Africa, has seen the number of people living in extreme poverty almost double.
>
> (WEF 2015)[8]

Fourth, there is the incongruous structure of the global economy, in which several countries are heavily invested in the production and export of fossil fuels even though current extraction and processing are unsustainable because they conflict with the stability of the Earth's climate. This difficulty is worsened by the fact that some oil-dependent economies have few alternative exportables while, at the same time, large industries have been built around fossil fuels and they are unwilling to accept losses or the taxes and other charges that would be needed to fund the transition to a new global energy matrix.

Choosing inaction

Instead of supporting immediate reductions in the production and consumption of fossil fuels, most businesses, governments, politicians, journalists, and economists prefer to deny climate change, or to exaggerate the potential and underestimate the costs of geoengineering and carbon sequestration initiatives.[9] The wish to postpone meaningful action until it becomes profitable for individual businesses to change their technologies and output mixes has been accompanied by the continuing rejection of regulation and taxes to finance the prevention and mitigation of climate change.[10] In the meantime, country-level negotiations proceed with their trademark lethargy; there, delegations slowly squabble their way toward policies, treaties, and laws that will deliver too little, far too late. In choosing this course of action, global capital and AE governments willingly bypass the fact that the required technologies will not be available for several years, and that it would be reckless to tamper with the atmosphere through geoengineering while continuing to pump growing quantities of CO2e into the air.

The dominant approach to climate policy attempts to preserve current lifestyles and leave untouched powerful industries, especially oil, while aiming to address environmental change through the creation of *other* profitable industries:[11]

> [E]very energy model reviewed for this Report concludes that it is impossible to get onto the 2°C trajectory with only energy efficiency and the diffusion of existing technologies. New or emerging technologies, such as carbon capture and storage, second-generation biofuels, and solar photovoltaics, are also critical. Few of the needed new technologies are available off the shelf. Ongoing carbon capture and storage demonstration projects currently store only about 4 million tons of CO_2 annually. Fully proving the viability of this technology in different regions and settings will require about 30 full-size plants at a total cost of $75 billion to $100 billion. Storage capacity of 1 billion tons a year of CO_2 is necessary by 2020 to stay within 2°C warming.
>
> (WDR 2010, p. 16)

Needless to say, those targets for storage capacity were not achieved (Consoli and Wildgust 2017). The mainstream approach to geoengineering and carbon storage resembles the (typically neoliberal) idea that the best way to address the obesity epidemic is by offering subsidised bariatric surgery in private hospitals while, at the same time, leaving untouched the existing systems of provision of food and the drivers of overconsumption, or, alternatively, the notion that the best way to tackle the stresses of contemporary life is by facilitating the prescription of antidepressants, instead of recognizing that neoliberalism is incompatible with human health and happiness. This is also why the so-called "debate" about the harmful effects of tobacco was kept alive for decades—merely to allow the cigarette manufacturers to profit for longer from driving their best customers (literally) into the ground (which was not a significant drawback, as long as new patrons could be found to replace the defunct ones). In the meantime, the world burns. In a nutshell, today, debates around geoengineering are, in practice, little more than an excuse to stall reductions in CO2e emissions.

Finally, it is important to reject the notion that climate change benefits one age group ("the old") at the expense of another ("the young"). This fantasy aims to place at the center of the debate a presumed conflict between age cohorts, but this is a diversion for three reasons. First, "old" and "young" are blurry categories that include those who have consumed far too much CO2e throughout their lives (generally the rich and those from the Global North) and those who have never consumed enough of anything (the poor and most people in the Global South): some people have enjoyed wasteful lives, while others have been deprived of almost everything that makes human existence materially easy. Also, while some individuals have chosen to ignore their impact on the environment, others are committed to salvaging life on Earth, and so on. Second, everyone who is lucky enough to live a full life goes through a sequence of ages. Pitting the young against the old is meaningless, since today's youngsters will inevitably "change sides" at some point, whatever their views and attitudes, undermining the facile opposition on which the analysis is built. Third, old people suffer disproportionately from respiratory illnesses and other consequences of pollution; they are highly vulnerable to climate-induced illness and premature death, highly reliant on fragile health services, and so on, which destabilizes the notion that the elderly systematically "exploit" the young or live "at the expense of" the young, or that the wanton behavior of today's old, decades ago, is the cause of this year's forest fires or next season's hurricanes.

The inaction of most governments and political leaders has been driven by worse motives than those of the proverbial ostrich, which idiotically refuses to see what it dislikes. Global businesses are making money from the depredation of the Earth's conditions to support life, while they demand even *higher* profits in order to reduce the damage that they inflict on the planet. The word "blackmail" comes to mind, except that, in mainstream economics, this is called "profit maximization." Wealthy Norway, a major oil producer, offers a particularly egregious example of self-interested inaction:

> [A] consistent thread of Norway's climate policy ... is the notion that climate change should be addressed only at the point of emissions, while the supply of fossil fuels should be left to the market. That view is now no longer supportable ... There are two elements to this argument: first, that reducing Norwegian production will not affect global emissions because other countries will replace the production; and second, that production in Norway has lower emissions. The first is at best misleading, and the second misses the point ... The claim that others will replace any reduced Norwegian production refers to a problem known as leakage: reduced supply in one place pushes up the oil price, making more expensive production viable somewhere else ... The same is true when tackling emissions at source ... reducing oil demand (for example, by making vehicles more efficient) decreases the price, encouraging consumers elsewhere in the world to increase their consumption. The key question is on which side climate action leaks more? ... Statistics Norway examined this question ... [and] ... recommended that in order to achieve maximum climate benefit at lowest cost ... the majority of climate mitigation should take place on the supply side.
>
> (McKinnon et al. 2017, pp. 15, 19)

The distributional implications of climate change are stark, both within and between countries. For example:

> When market failures take the form of environmental externalities, why do the institutions of governance fail to remedy them? There are three possible reasons: First, the losers may belong to future generations who are not here to defend themselves. In such cases, the only remedy for governance failure is a social commitment to an ethic of intergenerational responsibility. Second, the losers may lack adequate information as to the extent or sources of environmental burdens ... In such cases, environmental education and right-to-know legislation are crucial elements of a solution. Third, the losers may lack sufficient power to alter the behavior of the winners. In such cases, a change in the balance of power between winners and losers is a necessary condition for greater environmental protection.
>
> Boyce (2004, p. 11)[12]

Having fudged the costs and adverse distributional implications of climate change, the mainstream view plays its last card: it claims that climate change carries significant uncertainties that would complicate the tasks of mitigation and adaptation; moreover, the economy tends to grow and technologies improve all the time. Therefore, it is better to do nothing today, wait for climate change to play itself out, and then try to mitigate the outcomes. This argument is misleading, because those relatively smooth calculations can be thrown off-course entirely by climate unknowns, thresholds, and tipping points, which can have catastrophic implications.

Financialization and the climate

The tensions, dislocations, environmental stresses, and regressive distributional outcomes outlined above were intensified by the financialization of global production, exchange and social reproduction in recent decades.[13]

Financialization is not merely one among many factors explaining the rise of today's global(ized) economy; instead, it is the main driver and the key distinguishing feature of the neoliberal system of accumulation. Financialization is defined by the increasing significance of finance, financial institutions, and financial markets (what Marx called "interest-bearing capital," IBC) on social and economic reproduction. Their influence takes place through the control by IBC of the main sources of capital, foreign exchange, and state finance; the processes of resource allocation; and the main levers of economic policy in contemporary economies. At the same time, the ideologies associated with finance have become hegemonic in the media, research institutions, universities, and the state itself to such an extent that they are the "common sense" of our age. In policy terms, the hegemony of finance generally appears under the guise of "macroeconomic stabilization," "inflation control," and the "promotion of competitiveness," which have become prominent policy principles under neoliberalism. Finally, individual behaviors have also become financialized through the roll-back of the welfare state accompanied by rising levels of personal debt, and through the widespread calculation of "profits" and "losses" in the choice of profession, home, school, university, car, household appliance, and so on.

Financialization has led to dysfunctional outcomes, including short-termist and speculative accumulation strategies; macroeconomic volatility; low rates of investment, productivity growth, saving, GDP growth, and employment creation; vulnerability to crises; and mounting inequalities in income, wealth, power, and social provisioning (Lavoie 2014; Serfati 2003). Under financialization, the dominant economic interests operate in fragmented and competitive markets bound to a logic of procyclical investment and rapid profit extraction that tends to reinforce existing economic structures, lock in oil dependence, raise emissions, and block mitigation and adaptation. This makes financialization incompatible with high-cost, long-term, co-ordinated industrial policies; structural transformations in economic activity; economic diversification; the emergence of new drivers of accumulation; adaptation and mitigation of climate change; and the redistribution of income, as opposed to its capture by those who already control most resources (Chesnais 2016; Heynen et al. 2007; Hudson 2010).

The distortions imposed by financialization explain why the financial system continues to fund environmentally damaging initiatives that conflict with internationally agreed-upon emissions targets, and that will expand the bundle of assets that must be stranded (abandoned, or kept in the ground) when the world finally shifts away from fossil fuels (see Chapter 2 and Ansari and Holz 2020; Bos and Gupta 2019; Jakob and Hilaire 2015; McGlade and Ekins 2015; Raval et al. 2020; Vercelli 2017):

> The Paris Climate Agreement's target … will require a rapid decarbonization of the global energy system. Distressingly, levels of fossil fuel financing … [by] banks between 2013 and 2015 are incompatible with these … targets:
>
> **Coal mining** – … [T]op banks financed \$42.39 billion for companies active in coal mining, led by **Deutsche Bank** with \$6.73 billion.
> **Coal power** – In spite of a recent study concluding that the current pipeline of planned coal power plants would put the 2°C climate target out of reach … these banks financed \$154 billion for top operators of coal power plants, led by **Citigroup** with \$24.06 billion.
> **Extreme oil (Arctic, tar sands, and ultra-deep offshore)** – Future development of most of these high-cost, high-risk oil reserves is incompatible with even the 2°C target, but banks financed \$307 billion for the top owners of the world's untapped "extreme oil" reserves, led by **JPMorgan Chase** with \$37.77 billion.
> **Liquefied Natural Gas (LNG) export** – Banks financed \$283 billion, led by **JPMorgan Chase** with \$30.58 billion, for companies involved with LNG export terminals in North America, which have enormous carbon footprints and are stranded assets in the making based on a 2°C climate scenario.
>
> (Fossil Fuel Report Card 2016, p. 3)

Even worse: between 2016 and 2019, the top 35 private banks advanced US$2.7 trillion in credits to the fossil fuel industry (Fossil Fuel Finance Report 2020). These initiatives are irrational even from the point of view of the long-term interests of capital:

> [T]he most expensive and environmentally destructive forms of oil— tar sands, Arctic drilling and ultra-deepwater drilling— … [offer] the worst prospects. The very high cost of projects in these subsectors make them likely to end up as stranded assets as carbon regulations come online in the coming years. Effectively, any major extreme oil project is a huge bet that the world won't address climate change
> (Fossil Fuel Report Card 2016, p. 27)[14]

This is unacceptable from the perspective of the preservation of life on Earth, and it illustrates the argument that financialization is incompatible with democratic values and human equality.[15] This should be sufficient reason to reverse financialization; but when these ethical imperatives are coupled with the fact that neoliberalism and financialization intensify the challenges to life itself, it becomes clear that there is an urgent need to transform the structures of economic reproduction, reverse financialization and neoliberalism, diversify economies, promote environmental adaptation and mitigation, and achieve greater equality within and between countries.

Notes

1 For an overview, see IPCC Working Group I (2018); McKibben (2011b); and WDR (2010). For the environmental and health implications of coalburning, see https://www.ucsusa.org/resources/coal-and-air-pollution#. V74QyqI2Ymg.
2 See also Baer 2012.
3 Khor et al. (2017) review the mandate and achievements of the UNFCCC.
4 "[T]he absolute growth of GDP is the best predictor of the change in emissions. The only periods in which the greenhouse emissions that are destroying the stability of the Earth climate declined have been the years in which the world economy ceased growing and contracted, i.e. during economic crises. From the point of view of climate change, economic crises are a blessing, while economic prosperity is a scourge. This paradoxical reality is either ignored or actively denied by most economists, politicians and intellectuals of different fields and disciplines" (Granados 2018, p. 23; see also Le Quéré et al. 2020; and Rezai and Stagl 2016).
5 See https://www.iea.org/data-and-statistics, http://www.globalcarbonatlas. org/en/CO2-emissions and Jorgenson (2014).
6 https://theconversation.com/eighteen-countries-showing-the-way-to-carbon-zero-112295.

7 https://www.bbc.co.uk/news/world-us-canada-50165596.

8 See also WDR 2010.

9 There are "immense obstacles to the building of CCS [carbon capture and sequestration] plants ... As the energy analyst Vaclav Smil has pointed out: 'In order to sequester just a fifth of current CO_2 emissions we would have to create an entirely new worldwide absorption-gathering-compression-transportation-storage industry whose annual throughput would have to be about 70 percent larger than the annual volume now handled by the global crude oil industry, whose immense infrastructure of wells, pipelines, compressor stations and storage took generations to build.' CCS technology requires unimaginable quantities of water ... And the problems only start there, since the larger technological, economic, and ecological obstacles to such massive attempts at negative-emissions technologies are gargantuan ... [S]imilar problems of scale arise with respect to the most favored carbon dioxide removal approach among scientists, since it is theoretically capable of providing negative emissions, namely, Bio-energy with Carbon Capture and Sequestration (BECCS). Implementation of such schemes on a global scale would ... require a very large portion of the land area and water currently used by world agriculture, imposing intolerable environmental and social costs. More rational schemes propose improved agriculture and forestry, rooted in agroecology, for which Cuba is currently the most developed model" (Foster and Clark 2020, p. 280; see also Sapinski et al. 2020).

10 Granados zooms in on a crass example of poor economics: "Decades ago stupid economists developed the theory of the so-called environmental Kuznets curve, which asserted that with economic growth and increasing affluence environmental problems get worse at first, but then improve. Applied to climate change, the environmental Kuznets curve for greenhouse gasses ... states that continuous economic growth will eventually reduce emissions of CO_2 so that, eventually, with the market economy left to its own devices, climate change will cease to be a problem. The reality was, however, that worldwide emissions continued to grow, and the faster the world economy expanded, the faster they grew" (Granados 2018, p. 26; see also Ackerman et al. 2012; Boyce 2004; Hickel 2020; and Nuroglu and Kunst 2018).

11 "Contrary to the platitudes of most economists and almost all politicians who either deny the problem (like Trump) or tell us it is not that difficult to solve it with some technical innovations and policies (like Obama, Gore, and the heads behind the European Emission Trading System), only policies affecting the way things are produced and consumed at large, in the whole world economy, would be able to cut greenhouse gas emissions to a degree that could be effective to prevent catastrophic climate change. But if these policies were put in place, they would largely affect the consumption of individuals. It is inconceivable to prevent catastrophic climate change if airplanes, cars, international commerce, meat production and deforestation continue throwing hundreds million tons of CO_2 and CH_4 (methane), the two most important greenhouse gases, to the atmosphere" (Granados 2018, p. 25).

12 "With mitigation costs estimated to add up to \$4 trillion to \$25 trillion over the next century, the losses implied by such delays are so large that

there are clear economic benefits for high-income countries committed to limiting dangerous climate change to finance early action in developing countries. More generally, the total cost of mitigation could be greatly reduced through well-performing carbon-finance mechanisms, financial transfers, and price signals" (WDR 2010, p. 12).

13 For a historical overview, see Gowan (1999); Panitch and Gindin (2012); and Saad-Filho (2017). Theories of financialization are examined by Arrighi (1994); Ashman and Fine (2013); Christophers and Fine (2019); Fine (2013–2014); Fine and Saad-Filho (2017); and Saad-Filho (2018). For data and regularly updated analyses, see various issues of UNCTAD's *Trade and Development Report*.
14 See also later issues of this report and Grant 2020.
15 See Beaverstock et al. (2013) for the rise of the super-rich and their access to financial products; see also Goda and Lysandrou (2013) and Lysandrou (2018).

2 The imperative to change

This chapter examines the imperative to adapt and change the systems of economic production and social reproduction in order to protect the possibility of life as we know it. In confronting perhaps the most momentous challenge that our species has ever faced, it is essential to identify the features of the problem in the Global South and the Global North. It is also imperative to address the question of energy transition and the future size and shape of the oil industry. Whatever solution is eventually found, it will inevitably require stranding a large part of the known reserves of fossil fuels, with significant costs to be allocated for many years to come.

Transitions north and south

The Global North, with one-sixth of the world's population, is the source of almost two-thirds of the greenhouse gases in the atmosphere (Ackerman et al. 2012; WDR 2010). It is obvious that effective action to address climate change must rely primarily on the North. There, policies can focus on three main areas: reductions in consumption through cuts in disposable income and coordinated reductions in output; changes in production, finance, and consumption in order to lower the environmental damage per dollar of income; and shifting the energy matrix from fossil fuels to renewables, including leaving fossil fuels in the ground (Boyce 2004; Gençsü et al. 2020; Hahnel 2012).[1] There is no question that decarbonization will be difficult to achieve even in the wealthiest economies. For example:

> [M]oving beyond oil will be a challenge for Norway, where it currently accounts for 12 percent of the country's GDP and 13 percent of government revenue … By comparison, in Angola … oil accounts for 40 percent of GDP and 70 percent of government

revenue. Not only is Norway less dependent than many other major producers, but it also has significantly more resources (income and wealth) to facilitate the transition … Given finite global carbon budgets, each barrel of oil extracted in Norway is a barrel that cannot be extracted elsewhere. The likely result is depriving poor countries of development opportunities: essentially of revenue that could be used to build hospitals or schools … When Oil Minister Terje Soviknes says "It won't be possible to replace the [Norwegian] revenue stream from oil and gas for several more generations," that is a claim either that the rest of the world must suffer climate change, or that poorer countries should bear more of the burden of transition than wealthy Norway.

(McKinnon et al. 2017, pp. 4, 17)

Diversification, structural change, and mitigation are more manageable in the Global North than in the Global South, because the AEs have higher productivity across most sectors, and their economies tend to be more diversified and resilient. The AEs can more easily fund investment in sustainable energy sources and services, build alternative supply chains, and so on. However, in order to secure social and political support for the transition, it will be necessary to find alternative employment opportunities with comparable incomes for the workers dislocated by the transition.[2] In summary, the AEs should implement an aggressive strategy of divestment from fossil fuels, economic diversification, and social protection, and they should support parallel transitions in the South (McKinnon et al. 2017; World Bank 2017).

The challenges posited by climate change will weigh more heavily—both per capita and in proportion to national income—on poorer and less diversified economies. In particular, poor oil-export-dependent economies will become unable to rely on their established competitive advantages to achieve macroeconomic, external, fiscal, distributional, and other balances, and for employment generation, income, consumption, productivity growth, and social welfare (UNFCCC 2005). For many economies, these resources are significant—for example, the total rents captured by developing countries in 2012 were five times larger than the aid flows to the South (Morrissey 2016).[3]

Poor countries will find it difficult to absorb those costs and losses, and fund the required investments, especially in view of the urgency of these tasks and the large externalities involved (ETC 2018; Manley et al. 2017). This is because the DEs suffer from multiple disadvantages, including low capital stocks, outdated technologies, and less efficient education and training, which lead to lower productivity and lower incomes. Their markets are also smaller, and they are more vulnerable to adverse shocks; moreover, several DEs depend on a small number of exportables, often with high carbon content. Finally, the poorest oil-export-dependent countries will have to forgo, quite soon, much of their potential wealth as part of the worldwide transition (see Chapter 3). They will need support to transform their economies and address the consequences of climate change in the little time available. Forms of support can include aid, subsidized loans, technology transfers, and—importantly—favorable global regulations.[4]

Given the heavy costs of adaptation, mitigation, and transition both now and into the future, the DEs have stressed the need to protect their R2D, which has been already been enshrined in a myriad of UN resolutions and by the UNFCCC (Khor et al. 2017). R2D underpins the notion of CBDR, by which

> some countries are both more responsible for climate change and have a greater capacity to reduce their emissions … This idea is captured in the notion of "common but differentiated responsibilities," by which all countries have a responsibility to reduce their emissions, but those responsibilities are differentiated so that the greatest share of the burden falls on advanced industrial economies.
>
> (Morrissey 2016)

CBDR implies that the AEs must bear the greatest share of the burden of mitigation, both because of their historical responsibility for emissions and because they control much greater financial and technological resources today. The AEs have pushed back against these demands, claiming that they are already reducing emissions while the DEs are still expanding theirs, so the burden should be shared more evenly.[5] The DEs reject this argument, stating that it would be inadmissible to limit their growth when the AEs enjoyed a free run in the past; moreover, much of the emissions cuts in the North were due to the relocation of "their" carbon-intensive and heavily polluting production to the South (see Chapter 1). Because of tensions and disputes such as these, few countries have been willing to lead the way on emissions cuts; moreover, the best-performing economies are not among the greatest emitters of CO2.

Countries in the South have expressed concern with property rights and the pricing of carbon emissions in international agreements. For example:

> The principle of allocations pegged to historic emission levels, which was applied to industrialized countries in the Kyoto agreement,

effectively "grandfathers" these rights on the basis of past appro-priation. This formula is naturally unacceptable to the developing countries, whose emissions per capita remain an order of magni-tude below those in the industrialized countries. An alternative principle would be to allocate rights on the basis of equal per capita entitlements ... [An] egalitarian resolution would make global environmental governance and instrument for reducing North-South disparities.

(Boyce 2004, p. 18)

Finally, there is the vexed matter of the distribution of revenues from a (to be imposed) global carbon tax, which, if poorly designed, "could make the cost of access to modern energy sources prohibitive [in the Global South], increase poverty incidence and the use of non-priced resources by the poor" (Khor et al. 2017, p. 5).

Across all these areas of dispute, there is no question that the South must seek to self-fund their strategies of mitigation, adaptation, and transition as much as possible, as opposed to depending on transfers from the North, important as they may be (see Chapter 7). This autonomy could be facilitated—somewhat paradoxically—by continu-ing oil extraction, on the grounds that most countries in the South are small, their output is tiny relative to global demand, and they do not yet have alternative sources of foreign exchange, meaning that any shortfalls of hard currency due to rapid cuts in oil exports would create hardship, unless they were compensated by additional Northern aid (see Chapter 7). In these circumstances, it may be acceptable for small countries to finance their transition to a more diversified and oil-free future through a first-priority claim on (to be introduced) global extraction quotas:

[W]e could burn virtually all of the fossil fuel reserves in the developing world [excluding China], *and we would still have a 50% chance of keeping global temperature rise below 1.5°C* ... The total value of these reserves is ... thought to be ... *around $21 trillion* ... These resources ... represent a significant opportunity for improv-ing the lives of some of the world's poorest people, and they can be exploited without necessarily inducing dangerous levels of climate change.

(Morrissey 2016)

These difficulties would increase further if the principle of CBDR were applied to stranding part of the known reserves of fossil fuels, which would create accounting losses of hundreds of billions of dollars to countries and corporations; this would also imply the scrappage of tens of billions of dollars of productive capital in the extractive and processing industries, the elimination of millions of jobs, and the closure (not merely mothballing) of mines, oil platforms, refineries, ports, and so on. To these losses must be added the investments needed to change the world's energy matrix away from fossil fuels while, simultaneously, retrofitting our way of life to make it compatible with negative emissions, plus the costs of mitigating climate change, since it can no longer be avoided entirely. These costs will require compensatory funding as well as worldwide changes in legislation and accounting rules (Khor et al. 2017; Morrissey 2016). Nevertheless, action must be taken soon because the shock will be even worse if, instead of a managed decline of fossil fuel consumption, a sudden collapse in the demand for oil triggers unmanageable losses in many corporations and countries and, almost inevitably, a global economic crisis.

This process will not be straightforward. In the recent past, Bolivia and Ecuador made pioneering attempts to strand some of their reserves of fossil fuels in the expectation of external funding, but they failed almost entirely to raise resources (Arsel et al. 2016). This does not bode well for future attempts to redistribute the costs of stranding vastly larger oil-related assets in several countries simultaneously (see, for example, Corbera et al. 2019; Detchon and Van Leeuwen 2014; Greenleaf 2019; Joslin 2019; Hall 2004; He 2019; McElwee et al. 2019; Muradian et al. 2013; Nelson et al. 2019; Ouedraogo 2020; Sander and Cranford 2010; Shapiro-Garza 2019).

In addition to the distributional challenges between countries, outlined above, the rich must settle their ecological debt vis-à-vis the poor in each country. This notional debt has been incurred because, in each society, the wealthy have historically consumed disproportionately larger volumes of resources per capita, destabilising the ecosystem and imposing a large carbon footprint on society as a whole. The implication is that society is owed compensation, which can be settled through high taxes on luxury goods, polluting corporations, fossil-fuel-consuming activities, and so on.

Steps forward

Addressing climate change will require both international agreements and domestic policy shifts. The policy alternatives are examined in Chapters 4–7. International agreements will be needed in several areas, including (a) financial transfers to the South, in line with R2D and

CBDR, to cover the costs of stranding, mitigation, and transition; (b) the transfer of green technologies to the South, including global pools for environmental goods and technologies; (c) carbon pricing and taxes, and appropriate rules and channels for the collection and distribution of the revenues (Khor et al. 2017; Sekar et al. 2019a); and (d) new institutions for global environmental governance, which could follow three pathways (Boyce 2004). First, and most strongly, a new World Environmental Organisation (WEO) tasked with the protection of the environment, mitigation policies and transfers to the South. This is the most desirable pathway, but there is limited appetite for it in the North. This can be evidenced by the fate of the United Nations Environment Programme, whose mandate has been limited to information and assistance, and does not extend to policymaking. Second, in the absence of the WEO, there may be issue-specific agreements under the UNFCCC or even the WTO in order to address environmental threats, mirroring the agreements around nuclear proliferation and the protection of whales (hopefully avoiding their respective loopholes). Third is the attempt to "green" existing international institutions and agreements, that is, to bring environmental considerations into their decision-making processes, beyond often formal environmental impact assessments.[6]

Two areas are crucial. The first is carbon-pricing, in order to encourage emissions cuts:

> In almost any scenario that envisions meeting the ... UNFCCC global greenhouse gas emissions targets one of the more accepted and frequently considered policy options to achieve this goal is to put a price on carbon ... [S]ome jurisdictions have moved ahead and established carbon trading or carbon taxation frameworks, including Canada, Costa Rica, Norway, and Australia. South Africa, for instance, is implementing its second draft carbon tax that ... would cover all GHG emissions relating to the production of energy and non-energy industrial processes at the rate of 120 rand per metric ton (or approximately 8 USD) ... There is no single approach to carbon pricing that will work for every jurisdiction, and similarly, not all jurisdictions manage revenues from carbon levies equally. Some approaches focus on re-investing in low carbon technologies and practices, while others focus on using these funds to support vulnerable communities and industry.
>
> (Sekar et al. 2019a, p. 9)

However, since this would raise production prices, it would put compliant countries at a competitive disadvantage, unless there were global compensatory mechanisms in place. Second, then, is international coordination both to avoid free-riding and to deal with the externalities that are due to the global nature of the Earth's climate. The counterpart to international coordination is the need for incentives for firms to adopt "green" technologies, which are essential from a global point of view, but inevitably costly for individual companies. At both levels, treaties, domestic regulation, and state incentives are imperative (Sekar et al. 2019a). In summary, there are huge potential gains from policy coordination, but they require international agreements; in contrast, reliance on the pricing mechanism, although important, may not lead to significant progress within the relevant time-frame. Instead, it will be essential to mobilize collective action within and outside the state, in order to neutralize the corrosive influence of well-funded interests and their professional lobbies. These goals will not be easy to achieve, and policy implementation will be fraught. Confronting these challenges will require political will and determination to succeed.[7] The selfish and short-termist logic of neoliberalism and financialization will detract from these collective goals, showing, again, that they must be confronted head-on (see Chapter 4).

The energy transition and the (unavoidable) devaluation of oil-related resources will have an uneven impact on global economic growth. The scrappage of assets, technologies, jobs, and ways of living will tend to slow down growth, while large "green" investments in energy and infrastructure can create jobs, promote rapid sustainable growth, and generate resources for redistribution (Newell and Simms 2019). Given the costs and externalities involved, and the disparities of income, capabilities, and technology between North and South and rich and poor, and the historical responsibility for emissions by the North and by the rich in each country, it follows that the costs of addressing climate change, mitigation, and investment in diversification must be distributed fairly. Bizarrely, for example, "[s]witching from SUVs to fuel-efficient passenger cars in the U.S. alone would nearly offset the emissions generated in providing electricity to 1.6 billion more people" (WDR 2010, p. 3). This seems to be especially low-hanging fruit, until one realizes that this fruit has never been picked. This does not bode well for the harder efforts that must be made at other levels in order to cut emissions. In the meantime, most of the world's population continues to suffer from poverty, multiple deprivations, preventable diseases, and other ills. Improvements in living standards and the redistribution of income, wealth, and power are morally and politically imperative, but they have been blocked by social, economic, and political constraints.

The precise costs of transition are uncertain, but they need not be overwhelming. For example, Ritchie (2017) reports total global costs of climate mitigation of €200–€350 billion per year by 2030, which is less than 1% of the forecasted global GDP, plus upfront investments of €530 billion in 2020 (by now obviously unrealistic), or €810 billion if action is delayed to 2030 (alternatively, Ackerman et al. 2012 report required investments of US$1 trillion per year for sustainability). Even though these figures are substantial in absolute terms, the cost of inaction is likely to be much higher, with an expected 40% increase in mitigation costs for each decade of delay (Furman and Podesta 2014). Rapid economic growth can support those efforts, although success is not guaranteed (see Chapter 5).

Notes

1 For the case against "keeping it in the ground," see IER (2016) and KinderMorgan (2020).
2 "Protecting the livelihoods of those workers and their families must be a priority in the transition away from the oil economy. However, that does not diminish the need to make the transition. As the International Trade Union Confederation puts it, 'there are no jobs on a dead planet'" (McKinnon et al. 2017, p. 20).
3 Rents are usually defined as the difference between world prices and local costs of production; for the simplest possible example, if the international oil price is US$75/barrel and Saudi Arabian oil can be extracted for US$10/barrel, Saudi rents will be US$65/barrel. Here, rents are resources gifted by the world to low-cost producers by virtue of their favorable natural endowments or control of market supply or demand. These resources can be used for any purpose, for example, higher consumption or investment. From another angle, in mainstream economic theory rent is the return to a factor of production above the amount necessary to bring that factor into use; alternatively, rents are the returns exceeding those accruing from the next-best alternative use of a factor of production (e.g., the production of an alternative crop in the same land, or investment in agriculture as opposed to mining). Finally, rents can also be seen as returns exceeding the competitive cost of production (in the example above, the sale of oil above the domestic extraction cost). From this viewpoint, "rents" are always due to market distortions in relation to the perfectly competitive ideal.
4 "The rapid introduction of new sectors and products that expand the use of clean energy and improve efficiency are both in the national and global interest. But their rapid propagation could be hindered by response measures that obstruct development of the same sectors by other countries. For example, when strong intellectual property protections prevent adaptive activities and reverse engineering or when the prices of goods for the new technology are subsidized in the same way that agricultural products from developed countries are today" (Khor et al. 2017, p. 4; see also pp. 2–3).
5 For comparisons, see http://www.globalcarbonatlas.org/en/CO2-emissions.

6 Agreements can be reached to "[e]nsure that intellectual property rights ... [will] not be interpreted or implemented in a manner that limits or prevents any [country] from taking any measures to address environmental problems; ... establish global pools for environmental goods and technologies to promote effective global environmental action; ... [create] appropriate incentives, fiscal or otherwise, to stimulate the transfer of environmentally sound technology ... to developing countries; ... [a]dopt and enforce measures to provide differential royalty pricing between firms from developed and developing countries with respect to IPR-protected environmental goods and services ... [r]eview and amend all existing relevant national intellectual property rights regulations in order to remove the barriers and constraints affecting the transfer, absorption, and innovation of technology relating to environmental goods and the provision of environmental services in developing countries; [p]romote ... innovative intellectual property rights sharing arrangements for joint development of environmental goods and services among firms in developed and developing countries; [l]imit or reduce the minimum period of patent protection on environmental goods, including through appropriate amendment of TRIPS Article 33; [and] [p]rohibit 'ever greening' of patents with respect to environmental goods" (Khor et al. 2017, pp. 43–44).

7 "[T]he savings from helping to finance early mitigation in developing countries—for example, through infrastructure and housing construction over the next decades—are so large that they produce clear economic benefits for all. But designing, let alone implementing, an international agreement that involves substantial, stable, and predictable resource transfers is no trivial matter" (WDR 2010, p. 2).

3 The challenge of diversification

This chapter reviews the consequences of economic concentration and the case for diversification, focusing on oil-export-dependent countries. This argument is examined from different perspectives, including the economic distortions and vulnerabilities due to excessive concentration, the risks associated with the so-called "resource curse" and "Dutch disease," and the contrasting perspectives of different schools of economic thought. Finally, the chapter examines pathways toward diversification, focusing on the developing countries.

Economic concentration

Commodities can be grouped into three main families, due to their physical characteristics and economic linkages to the industrial sector. *Soft commodities* are mostly used in the food sector. They include cereals (such as wheat and rice), soya, beverages (such as tea and coffee), crops (such as cotton and timber), livestock (such as beef, pork, and lamb), and fish. *Hard commodities* comprise precious metals (such as gold and silver), ferrous metals (such as iron ore), non-ferrous metals (such as copper), and rare earth minerals (such as coltan). These commodities are generally used as inputs by the industrial and construction sectors, while precious minerals serve primarily as jewelry and reserve value. *Energy commodities* refer predominantly to fossil fuels (especially oil, gas, and coal). They are used across the spectrum, both as an intermediate and a final consumption good (Kaplinsky and Farooki 2012).

Economic concentration in the commodity sector is rarely defined precisely,[1] but it refers to the share of commodities of any family in employment, GDP, fiscal budgets, or exports (Dhir and Dhir 2015; UNCTAD 2019; UNFCCC 2005). Regardless of the nuances of definition, several DEs are obviously concentrated in and around fossil fuels. For example, in 2017 oil accounted for 99% of South Sudan's exports, 95% of Iraq's exports, and 84% of Angola's exports, while and oil and gas accounted for 80% of Nigeria's exports; oil rents reached 37% of GDP in Iraq, Kuwait, and Libya.[2] While some of these economies have used their fossil fuel exports to support comfortable lifestyles as well as some diversification (especially in the Gulf), others seem unable to sustain decent living standards, develop new industries, or extricate themselves from oil markets that are bound to collapse (Nigeria, Venezuela). Yet others lack plausible alternatives and would find it difficult to diversify (South Sudan).

Examination of the trade flows in commodity resources starts from the distinction between *resource abundance* and *resource dependence.* Abundance refers to resource endowments or the gross volume of production; the resources can be only an advantage for the country, since availability does not imply that these resources should or will be extracted; in contrast, actual exploration produces economic revenues. Finally, dependence refers to the importance of the resource sector to the generation of tax revenues, foreign exchange, growth, and employment, which may or may not be advantageous for an economy.

Various methods have been used to measure resource dependence. For Davis (1995), Lederman and Maloney (2012), and Sachs and Warner (1995), it refers to the share of primary commodities in either exports or GDP, or to resource exports per worker. Ding and Field (2005) measure resource dependence as the share of natural resources capital in total capital. Baunsgaard et al. (2012) define resource-dependent countries as those with oil, gas, and mineral revenues or exports of at least 20% of total fiscal or total export revenues, respectively, while Haglund (2011) uses a slightly higher threshold of 25% of total exports (Hailu and Kipgen 2017). A country can be resource-abundant but not resource-dependent (e.g., the United States, which is the largest oil and gas producer in the world), or vice-versa (e.g., Tanzania). For example:

> Both Central Asia and SSA [sub-Saharan Africa] exhibit high degrees of commodity dependence … Beginning with the contribution of commodities to GDP, the share of soft commodities … in output lies above the global average (4 percent) for both Central Asia (9 percent) and SSA (18 percent) … In both regions the contribution of mining … is above the global average of 6 percent. In Central Asia the share of the sector increased from 11 percent in 1992 to 15 percent in 2010, while it grew from 13 percent to 19 percent over the same period for SSA. By contrast, the

share of manufacturing in GDP is below the global average in both regions and has fallen over time ... The resource intensity of Central Asian and SSA economies is even more marked in the composition of their exports ... At the global level, manufactures account for the dominant share (58 percent) of world exports. By contrast ... the share of manufactures [in exports] rose from 19 percent to 23 percent [in Central Asia], while for SSA it decreased from 24 percent to 21 percent between 2000 and 2011. In both regions, hard and energy commodities account for a disproportionately large—and growing—share of exports. In Central Asia the share of fuel increased from 39 percent to 57 percent ... [while in] SSA ... [it] increased from 42 percent to 45 percent ... Associated with ... resource dependence ... is the ... small and declining contribution manufacturing makes to GDP in both regional economies, and the relatively low levels of technology in their industrial sectors.

(Kaplinsky and Farooki 2012, pp. 23–25, 28)

In order to measure the dependence of countries on natural resource extraction, Hailu and Kipgen (2017) developed the Extractives Dependence Index (EDI), including three indicators: (a) the share of export earnings from extractives in total export earnings; (b) the share of revenue from extractives in total fiscal revenue; and (c) the extractive industry value added in GDP. This is meant to capture three aspects of resource dependence—their contribution to export revenues, fiscal revenues, and GDP—while also taking into account the degree of specialization of the production structure that is due to resource dependence. Unsurprisingly, Hailu and Kipgen's (2017) calculation of the EDI for 81 countries shows extremely high values for such countries as Iraq, Libya, Angola, and the Democratic Republic of the Congo, and low values for the Philippines, the United Kingdom, Tunisia, and Vietnam.

Diversification in the orthodox and heterodox traditions

Debates around the advantages and disadvantages of specialization in the production and export of primary commodities have become part of the disputes between neoclassical and heterodox approaches to international trade. In brief, neoclassical trade theory is grounded in a static equilibrium approach to David Ricardo's (2014 [1821]) notion of comparative advantage as interpreted through the so-called "Heckscher-Ohlin" model. This model suggests that gains from trade are potentially ubiquitous, and they justify full economic specialization.

Using the traditional example of two countries (A and B), two goods (X and Y), and one factor of production (labor), if we assume that country A is relatively more efficient than country B at producing good X, and (by implication) that country B is relatively more efficient than A at producing Y, then each country's factors of production (in this case labor but, by extension, capital, land, technology, and anything else) should be entirely devoted to the production of the good in which that country enjoys a comparative advantage (in our example, country A should produce only X, and country B should produce only Y). Concentration in production should be supplemented by trade, by which each country's maximum potential output of *one* good can be translated into the maximum possible consumption of *all* goods.[3]

Schools of thought in heterodox economics have long challenged the mainstream's attachment to specialization and (consequently) rent capture. For the heterodoxy, even if economic concentration can be advantageous in the short term, specialization in the production of primary products tends to foster "rentier states" reliant on undependable external prices, and it can leave resource-dependent countries more vulnerable to shifts in technologies of production and patterns of consumption than countries with a diversified production structure (Hailu and Kipgen 2017; Hausmann and Hidalgo 2011; Hausmann and Klinger 2007). In addition, mineral resources are by definition finite, while agricultural products depend on the vitality of the soil, which can limit output. In addition, lack of economic diversification facilitates the leakage of income abroad through imports and capital flight, and it is associated with procyclical fiscal policies, macroeconomic volatility, boom and bust cycles, the long-term deterioration of the terms of trade, and other ills.[4] These patterns of production, employment, and consumption are likely to hamper long-term growth (ECLAC 2017; Hailu and Kipgen 2017).[5] It follows that developing countries should pursue policies of economic diversification for reasons of macroeconomic and balance of payments stability, resilience against shocks, sustained growth, and avoidance of risks of resource curse or Dutch disease (see below), and that they should do so to promote productivity growth, social welfare, and redistribution (Hesse 2008; Joya 2015).[6] Climate change would add another set of reasons for diversification, especially for fossil-fuel-dependent countries.[7]

The heterodoxy draws upon several scholarly traditions, especially the political economy of development associated with Friedrich List (1885 [1841]), the late developmentalism of Alexander Gerschenkron (1962), the structuralism of Raúl Prebisch (1950) and Hans Singer (1950), the evolutionary political economy of Alice Amsden (1997, 2001) and Ha-Joon Chang (1994), and closely related approaches. Albert Hirschman (1958) argued that, in DEs, the primary sector is dynamic and enjoys high productivity in the short term, but it offers poor long-term prospects for development; in contrast, the rest of the economy is initially weak but offers better opportunities for diversification and sustainable growth. Hirschman highlighted three main linkages between the economic sectors: he called them "fiscal," "consumption," and "production" linkages. Fiscal linkages concern the forcible harvesting of resources generated in the commodity sector through corporate taxes, royalties, and income taxes that may be transferred in order to support the development of sectors unrelated to primary commodities. Consumption linkages refer to the demand for the output of other sectors arising from the incomes earned in the commodities sector, which may foster investment in the domestic economy both directly and indirectly. Finally, production linkages refer to the chains of activities that connect firms and sectors within the economy. These linkages may be "backward" (through the production of inputs) or "forward" (through further processing) (Hailu and Kipgen 2017; Kaplinsky and Farooki 2012). Hirschman claimed that, in resource-abundant economies, the high productivity (primary) sector tends to have scant backward and forward production linkages with the rest of the economy (with mining as a prime example), as well as, often, limited capacity to create employment, drive productivity growth, or induce income growth (e.g., oil and agribusiness). Even worse, the combination of large foreign revenues and low employment in the competitive sector would tend to concentrate income and drive the rapid increase of the imports of inputs and luxury consumption goods, especially in periods of prosperity.

Hirschman was skeptical about the capacity of developing country governments to drive industrial development through fiscal linkages because, in his view, the mere existence of linkages did not provide guidance about which sectors should receive resource transfers to drive economic growth. He was less skeptical about consumption linkages, but since most resource-rich DEs had weak manufacturing sectors, Hirschman assumed that most income growth would leak abroad through imports (this is especially true in liberalized economies with scant barriers to trade). For Hirschman, the most viable avenue to economic diversification driven by commodity exports was through production linkages, especially backward linkages. He claimed that they provided both the guidance for the productive use of resources and the ready demand for them, paving the way to manufacturing growth and economic diversification.

In summary, despite their differences in focus and methodology, the heterodox approaches mentioned above have four features in common. First, they are not based on abstract-deductive reasoning, as is the case with the mainstream, which relies on simplistic assumptions about perfect markets, formal logic, and algebraic modeling to pass policy prescriptions. In contrast, heterodox views are grounded in an inductive and historically informed reading of the DEs, drawing upon case studies and the recognition of specific market failures.

Second, drawing upon historical studies, heterodox economists invariably claim that diversification, industrialization, and long-term economic growth are costly, and that they should build upon existing linkages and complementarities. Economic diversification can take place spontaneously; for example, the prosperity of coal mining creates demand for ports, connecting roads, fuel, service stations for trucks and machinery, food provision, entertainment services, and demand for public services, housing, and so on. Other linkages, potentially involving large capital investment and deeper and faster structural changes, can be promoted by the state through industrial policy (Szirmai 2012). Almost inevitably, these initiatives must be funded by the transfer of revenues from the successful (export) sector to new industries (Kaplinsky and Farooki 2012) and by the judicious use of external resources, especially loans and foreign investment (Brenton et al. 2019). These policy goals require sector-specific interventions rather than merely "horizontal" or non-sector-specific macroeconomic policy management.

Third, the potential advantages of diversification can be enhanced by greater income equality, because of its impact on social cohesion (as opposed to policy-disabling distributional conflicts), demand growth (since the poor tend to have a higher propensity to consume than the rich), and because higher wages create incentives for technological progress and the use of machinery in production.[8]

Fourth, industrialization can support the achievement of multiple developmental goals: greater economic independence, which would reinforce political independence (a crucial goal for postcolonial states in the Global South); employment creation (essential, given the rapid expansion of the workforce and the need to absorb surplus labor from agriculture); productivity growth (driven by the higher productivity in manufacturing vis-à-vis traditional agriculture, which is related to Verdoorn's Law); improved distribution of income and greater balance of payments stability, across the capacity to finance imports and debt repayments and reduce aid dependence; and, for the Structuralists, the scope to avoid the deterioration of the terms of trade (these arguments are related to the claim, associated with the work of Anthony

Thirlwall, that the balance of payments poses the most significant constraint to growth in the periphery).[9]

Despite these advantages, experience shows that it is difficult to diversify:

> Davis ... found that out of 23 mineral rich countries only Tunisia was able to diversify its economy in the period 1970–1991 ... [D] iversification seems to require a long period of structural changes. Furthermore, to the extent that countries should diversify, this is not an easy task as there are political constraints to doing so. Political interests and the type of state ... may affect the scope for attaining diversification.[10]
>
> (Wiig and Kolstad 2012, p. 197)

Historically, few economies have managed to diversify by following so-called "free market" policies. Instead, the successful experiences are concentrated among middle-income countries and those pursuing aggressive industrial policies (Mahroum and Al-Saleh 2016). Most poor countries with large reserves of fossil fuels have shown very limited capacity to diversify (Ahmadov 2012; Ait-Laoussine and Gault 2017; Alsharif 2017; Alsharif et al. 2017; Callen et al. 2014; Diop et al. 2012; Golub and Prasad 2016; Sen et al. 2019). Outcomes in this case tend to be even worse than those of hard-mineral-dependent economies (Gelb 2010; Ross 2017).

The literature suggests that key areas for successful diversification are regulations and investment policy, trade policy, competition policy, and financial flows (across domestic and international finance).[11] The current international division of labor points to the importance of export competitiveness for economic diversification and structural transformation. However, diversification is difficult in practice, since market forces tend to transfer resources toward sectors that are already relatively more productive, generally strengthening resource extraction further. It is also noticeable that countries that have diversified successfully have not generally addressed entrenched inequalities of income and wealth, among them Indonesia, Chile, and Malaysia (Esanov 2012; Zen 2011).

The theoretical and policy debates between mainstream and heterodox economists are highly relevant for DEs that have traditionally specialized in the production and export of primary commodities (for example, copper in Chile and Zambia, oil in Iraq and Nigeria, coffee in El Salvador and Uganda, sugar in Cuba, cotton in Uzbekistan, and gas in Bolivia). They have more limited relevance for the AEs, which have traditionally enjoyed a more diversified productive base, higher productivity, and greater competitiveness across manufacturing, agriculture, and services.

Diversification debates under neoliberalism

Heterodox views gained support in the literature between the 1950s and the early 1980s, and they gained support again in the mid-1990s. This was, in part, because they were perceived to have identified more precisely than the mainstream the drivers of growth in late developing countries, both those following import-substituting industrialization strategies (mostly in Latin America and Sub-Saharan Africa, as well as in India), and those following export-oriented industrialization (typically the East Asian Newly Industrializing Countries, NICs). The growing influence of heterodox views—albeit interrupted by the spread of neoliberalism between the early 1980s and the mid-1990s—was underpinned by the recognition that mainstream approaches inspired by the Washington Consensus (WC) had failed to address successfully the impact of the international debt crisis, and were unable to drive the resumption of growth in the affected DEs. Instead, mainstream adjustment polices became associated with one or even two "lost decades" across the Global South, in contrast with the achievements of different forms of developmentalism.

As is widely known,[12] the WC stresses the advantages of mainstream economic policies, including opening up to imports, devaluing the exchange rate, and "liberalizing" domestic markets. These policies are meant to compel local firms to become more efficient through the intensification of competition within the country (no "featherbedding") and against foreign producers. WC policies point toward greater specialization according to comparative advantage—that is, economic concentration as opposed to the allegedly "wasteful" diversification associated with developmentalism. For the mainstream, developing countries should also liberalize international flows of capital and their domestic financial systems in order to promote foreign investment; increase the availability of savings; and raise the rate of return to investments in their local economies.

Given the repeated failure of WC policies to foster rapid growth and the heavy criticisms levied by the heterodoxy, the mainstream sought to defend the WC through the repetition of neoclassical slogans, questionable appeals to the empirical evidence, selective reference to the occasional and invariably temporary (and always carefully promoted) "star performers," and the argument that the problem was not with its chosen policies but with the lack of "proper" implementation. This would open the way to discourses around corruption, bad governance, and the like, which seem to plague the Global South but not the Global North. These attempts to defend the WC were futile, and the post-Washington Consensus (PWC) was launched from within the World Bank in the second half of the 1990s. In terms of scholarship, both in intrinsic quality and external recognition, the PWC was far more powerful than its predecessor. Its success owed much to the talent and charisma of its pioneer, Joseph Stiglitz, even though he was removed from the position of Chief Economist at the World Bank by the US administration because of his critiques of International Monetary Fund (IMF) policies after the East Asian crisis.

The intellectual thrust of the PWC was to emphasize the significance of market and institutional imperfections, as opposed to the virtues of perfect markets promoted by the WC. Consequently, the PWC rejected the WC for its antipathy toward state intervention, while it also questioned conventional macroeconomic stabilization policies for their adverse short-term impact and long-term implications for distribution, diversification, and growth. The rhetoric of the PWC was state-friendly when contrasted with the WC, but in a limited and piecemeal way, with intervention being justified only on a case-by-case basis should it be demonstrable that narrow economic benefits would most likely accrue. Despite its obvious limitations, and its unstinting adherence to the mainstream theory of trade—and, consequently, the lack of emphasis on economic diversification—the PWC provided a rationale for discretionary intervention across a range of economic and social policies, while the WC offered none. However, the PWC remained fundamentally pro-market, favoring a (poorly examined) deepening of "globalization" (inevitably including economic concentration) but, ostensibly, with a more human face and guiding hand.

The most recent stage in these debates focused on the *prima facie* surprising attachment of the (otherwise heterodox) "Pink Tide" administrations in Latin America to the reprimarization of previously diversified economies during the global commodity boom and the period of fast growth in China and the United states between the early 2000s and the GFC ("neo-extractivism"). These gains were used to build the foundations of welfare states in one of the most unequal regions in the world (the "extractive imperative" for Arsel et al. 2016; see also Loureiro and Saad-Filho 2019). The expansion of primary production was noticed elsewhere too, even if it was less transformative of economic structures, for example in the United States (fracking), Sub-Saharan Africa (mineral and other resources), and Turkey (coal)

(Escaith and Tamenu 2014). Worryingly, the decline in commodity prices after 2011 may have reinforced the expansion of primary production worldwide because, once capital has been sunk in resource extraction, falling prices may intensify the pressure to extract more in order to stabilize revenue flows rather than create incentives for devaluation, scrappage of capital, diversification, and exit from the primary sector. At this level, too, "business as usual" remains the dominant model of development, regardless of the evidence in support of diversification and the mounting evidence of climate change.

Mainstream–heterodox debates around the advantages and costs of specialization were accompanied by two related controversies: first, around the so-called "resource curse" and the "Dutch disease" and, second, around reprimarization. In the late 1980s, mainstream economists counterintuitively suggested that dependence on natural resources (later expanded to include any other primary product, transport service, worker remittance, or development aid) tended to produce a range of economic ills (the "resource curse"), including low savings rates, slow GDP growth, currency overvaluation and misaligned exchange rates, high unemployment, high inflation and external debt, economic volatility (boom and bust cycles), political authoritarianism, corruption, and vulnerability to conflict.[13] The Dutch disease literature offers an even more pessimistic interpretation of resource dependence, drawing upon the experience of The Netherlands after the boom in offshore oil and gas in the 1970s. It was argued that the resource earnings overvalued the Dutch florin, with adverse consequences around deindustrialization and further concentration around the extractive sector.[14]

Heterodox economists soon pointed out that the "curse" and the "disease" depend almost entirely on the assumption of full employment. Once it is relaxed, the likelihood of adverse outcomes diminishes drastically, because the additional resource inflows can mobilize underutilized productive capacities and fund extra imports of goods and services, which can counter inflationary pressures and raise productivity. These policy options suggest that the "curse" and the "disease" are not unavoidable; instead, they are, ultimately, the consequence of misguided macroeconomic or industrial policies.

Approaches to diversification

It was shown above that economic diversification in DEs is imperative both for domestic reasons (resilience of the balance of payments, faster growth, lower volatility) and—especially in the case of oil-export-dependent countries—because of planetary imperatives (the limits of the global carbon budget). There is no room for new production, and a large share of the known reserves of fossil fuels can never be extracted. These pressures reinforce the desirability of economic diversification in order to increase resilience against climate change and to address the costs of mitigation (UNFCCC 2005).

The advantages of diversification are widely recognized in the policy-oriented (and, almost invariably, more pragmatic) literature:

> The world's poorest countries, many of which are often small or geographically remote, landlocked and/or heavily dependent on primary agriculture or minerals, tend to have the most concentrated economic structures. This creates challenges in terms of exposure to sector-specific shocks, such as weather-related events in agriculture or sudden price shocks for minerals ... Growth ... tends to be unbalanced in the case of mineral dependent countries or slow and difficult to sustain in agrarian ones. Poverty-reducing, trade-driven, growth has been particularly difficult to achieve in countries whose economies are heavily dependent upon primary commodities. Countries whose geography implies a punishing lack of connectivity to regional or world markets are also at a distinct disadvantage in attempting to diversify their product and export mix.
>
> (Brenton et al. 2019, pp. 136–137)[15]

Yet, beyond the essential political decisions and diplomatic negotiations stand the economists. In general, neoclassical economists claim that the "right" prices (incorporating scarcity, externalities, and so on), imposed through taxes, permits, or other forms of regulation, will be sufficient to direct resources toward technologies and patterns of consumption compatible with environmental protection. In contrast, heterodox economists tend to argue for greater caution and extensive state intervention on the grounds of uncertainty and precaution: the probabilities of specific outcomes are unknowable; innovations can fail or have unintended consequences; and the consequences of insufficient action now are so catastrophic that bold initiatives are imperative (Hansen et al. 2008; Hendrix 2017; Rezai and Stagl 2016).

Once the need for action at whatever speed has been agreed, two areas are especially significant: the transformation of energy supply toward renewables, and improvements in energy efficiency (Khor et al. 2017). Both involve disproportionate economic risks for the developing countries, over and above their social and political fragilities, as well as high costs for the fossil fuel industry (Sekar et al. 2019a). Here, higher carbon pricing and the likely collapse of demand as the global energy transition gains pace will affect poor countries in two ways. First, oil export-dependent countries may see a steep deterioration of their terms of trade, potentially skewing the global distribution of income to their disadvantage. Second, there will be significant distributional challenges within countries. Nevertheless, economic diversification is imperative, especially in the oil-export-dependent countries, both as part of the global energy transition and for these countries' own reasons.[16]

It was shown above that the rich in every country, and the richest economies worldwide, have profited disproportionately from the labor of others and from the bounty of the Earth, to the point of (possibly irreversibly) destabilizing the global environment. Given this track record, and the costs and complexity of successful transitions, it would be both unconscionable and ineffective to ask the poor and the poorest countries to shoulder the burden of changing economic strategies. In other words, the proposed solutions must be both technically efficient and socially fair, and economic diversification must contribute to the construction of democratic economies.

Difficulties of a different order emerge because the inevitable collapse in oil prices may take place suddenly—for example, when the fact that most reserves must be stranded is priced in, or when technological changes or demand shifts eventually collapse the market—with severe implications both domestically and globally (see Chapter 2). These constraints suggest that decisive action is needed both through country-level initiatives and multilateral co-operation, action embedded in treaties with much greater scope and ambition than those that have been attempted so far. Given previous disappointments, there is no mistaking the severity of these challenges.

The emerging consensus in the development literature is that diversification is generally good, "good policies" are key (despite the disagreements about their precise nature), and stabilizing institutions can help, for example, sovereign wealth funds. Beyond these certainties, the heterodoxy stresses the aggressive industrial policies deployed in the successful experiences of late development, in contrast with the continuing failure of non-diversified economies to achieve rapid and sustained growth or improvements in distribution. In contrast, the mainstream stresses the need for a specific set of macroeconomic policies that are traditionally associated with the WC and with the risks of political capture and corruption (Page 2008). The incompatibilities between this generic "pro-market" advice and the "resource curse" tend to be glossed over; distribution is generally bypassed; and the environmental constraint is often ignored.

The following chapters outline strategic and policy suggestions addressing the challenges of diversification, mitigation, and democratization of the economy, in order to lay the foundations for sustainability beyond neoliberalism.

Notes

1 "Economic diversification and growth of non-extractive sectors ... are important development objectives of resource-rich countries ... However, there is neither common definition of diversification nor metrics to measure it ... Most of the theories used to measure the level of economic diversification link it to levels of employment, exports or income. Economic diversification can be measured as the share of sectors in GDP, the share of sectors in exports (export concentration), the dependence of a country on the export of a good or commodity, and the employment share of sectors" (UNFCCC 2005, p. 19).

2 See Peszko et al. (2020), http://atlas.cid.harvard.edu/, and https://databank.worldbank.org/source/world-development-indicators#.

3 Alternatively, and appealing to barter and common sense: if you and I live together, and I am better than you at cooking and you are better than me at DIY, with all else constant our joint welfare will be maximized if you do all the DIY and I do all the cooking. The same static and non-monetary logic of full specialization holds in Ricardo's (2014 [1821]) famous example with two countries ("England" and "Portugal") and two goods ("cloth" and "wine"). Most mainstream textbooks demonstrate this notion using simple algebra (for a critique, see Shaikh 1979–1980).

4 "[M]any resource-dependent countries have a highly unbalanced tax base, especially oil dependent ones ... In 2010, tax revenues in the oil dependent SSA countries represented 30% of GDP, comparable to the OECD average of 33% of GDP. However, resource-related taxes represented an average of 73% of total taxes collected, ranging from 94% in Equatorial Guinea to 55% in Gabon. On average, non-extractives related corporate taxes made up just 6% of total tax revenues" (Hailu and Kipgen 2017, p. 255).

5 "[M]ainstream economics approaches to industrialization ... are centred on static comparative advantage and on tasking governments with imposing supply-side institutional reforms and improving governance so as to allow markets to perform more efficiently. Such a reading would ... be incorrect: after all, no country has managed to climb the industrial ladder just by 'getting prices and institutions right' ... [S]uccessful late-industrializing countries all feature 'activist' or 'developmental' states which—by going against capitalist logic and static comparative advantage—overtly mobilized resources and helped steer resource allocation to shape their country's future comparative advantage" (Storm 2017, pp. 1, 7).

6 "The world's poorest countries, many of which are often small or geographically remote, landlocked and/or heavily dependent on primary agriculture or minerals, tend to have the most concentrated economic structures. This creates challenges in terms of exposure to sector-specific shocks, such as weather-related events in agriculture or sudden price shocks for minerals ... Growth ... tends to be unbalanced in the case of mineral

dependent countries or slow and difficult to sustain in agrarian ones. Poverty-reducing, trade-driven, growth has been particularly difficult to achieve in countries whose economies are heavily dependent upon primary commodities. Countries whose geography implies a punishing lack of connectivity to regional or world markets are also at a distinct disadvantage in attempting to diversify their product and export mix" (Brenton et al. 2019, pp. 136–137; see also UNFCCC 2005 and Wiig and Kolstad 2012).

7 Paradoxically, in view of the extant literature Caselli et al. (2015) claim that exposure to international trade can reduce (rather than increase, as would normally be expected) macroeconomic volatility.

8 "[R]edistributing incomes from the high-income group (say the top 10 per cent) to the lower income groups (say the bottom 40 per cent) will not just raise domestic demand (because low-income earners spend more, and save less, per unit of income than the high-income earners); it will also provide a spur to productivity growth via higher investment, faster embodied technical progress and a deepening of the division of labour (meaning: greater industrial diversification)" (Storm 2017, p. 5).

9 For a contemporary example of a Structuralist argument: "Historically, the prices of globally traded commodities have not performed as well as those of globally traded manufactures, that is, the terms of trade have systematically turned against commodity exporting economies" (Kaplinsky and Farooki 2012, p. 10).

10 For examples of diversification, see Brenton et al. (2019); OECD (2011); and Woertz (2014).

11 For an overview, see Brenton et al. (2019); Hailu and Kipgen (2017); Kaplinsky and Farooki (2012); Mahroum and Al-Saleh (2016); and UNFCCC (2005).

12 For an overview, see Fine and Saad-Filho (2014); Jomo and Fine (2006); and Saad-Filho and Johnston (2005).

13 For a survey, see Saad-Filho and Weeks (2013); for the "resource curse," see Auty (2001); Carmignani and Mandeville (2014); Rosser (2006); and Sachs and Warner (1995). For the "Dutch disease," see Corden and Neary (1982). Collier and Hoeffler (2005) were the first to relate natural resource endowments and a propensity for civil conflict.

14 See Adam (2013) and Hailu and Kipgen (2017). For a contrasting viewpoint, see Fardmanesh (1991); Mikesell (1997); and, especially, Alexeev and Conrad (2009, p. 586), for whom "contrary to the claims made in several recent papers, the effect of a large endowment of oil and other mineral resources on a country's long-term economic growth has been on balance positive. Moreover, the claims of a negative effect of oil and mineral wealth on a country's institutions do not appear to be valid."

15 See also Ahrend 2008; Freire 2017; Hailu and Kipgen 2017; UNFCCC 2005; and Wiig and Kolstad 2012.

16 "What is clear is that economic diversification takes time. So a rational approach ... would be to begin that process now, while the production from existing fields gradually declines, rather than waiting until later, when the necessary changes would be abrupt, and hence much more difficult and costly" (McKinnon et al. 2017, p. 20; see also Peszko 2020).

4 Strategies for a democratic transition

This chapter outlines the principles of democratic economic strategies (DECS) and democratic economic policies (DEPs). They draw upon notions of social justice and inclusion, and on economic insights from the Post-Keynesian, Institutionalist, Evolutionary, Structuralist, Feminist, Kaleckian, and Marxian schools, as well as from other critical and ecological approaches to development economics. DECS and DEPs offer a compelling case for public policies focusing on diversification, manufacturing sector growth, sustainability, and improvements in social welfare and in the distribution of income, wealth, and power. Unavoidably, this requires systemic transitions away from neoliberalism and financialization. These transitions are at the core of the democratic strategy outlined in this chapter and in the chapters that follow.[1]

Democratic policies and strategies

DECS and DEPs build upon the pro-poor development (PPD) literature, which emerged in the early 2000s and which focused on the basic needs of the poor and on improvements in distribution.[2] DECS and DEPs add to these concerns the need to address climate change and the environmental constraint; they also claim that these drivers of change are mutually supportive and that they can underpin the ambition to build a democratic society transcending the limitations of neoliberalism.[3]

The "early" PPD literature attempted to confront the (P)WC by claiming that equity is an ethical imperative, and that both distribution and growth would benefit the poor. However, the tension between these two statements—one about principles (equality and gains for the poor) and the other about instruments (economic growth)—was exploited by the mainstream in a four-stage process. First, the mainstream conceded that equality is valuable. Second, it restricted the concept to equality of opportunity only. Third, it examined the relationship between growth and distribution through detailed measurements of the impact of (different types of) equality on growth, and found a set of useful correlations. Finally, it concluded that poverty and inequality are mutually reinforcing, and that what the World Bank called "inclusive growth" is the best way to address both of them simultaneously.

This containment strategy was successful for several reasons, but two were especially significant: the mainstream's vastly greater institutional resources, and the ill-advised inclination of the PPD camp to seek an accommodation with the mainstream. It was unwise to concede that any growth process that improves the lot of the poor is "pro-poor", because this conflates the definition of "pro-poor growth" with one of its indicators of success. This concession was the thin end of the wedge, since it disabled the principles of the PPD approach: the debate shifted to instruments. In retrospect, the scholars committed to PPD should have avoided a degenerating debate with the mainstream about the quantitative implications of (disembedded) growth processes upon absolute poverty and distribution. This was a mistake, because there is no growth "in general." *Growth exists only concretely*, as the outcome of economic strategies including specific fiscal, monetary, industrial, employment, balance of payments, and distributive and social policies.[4]

Since the modality of growth is inextricably bound up with its distributional and other outcomes, it makes no sense to examine the latter while leaving aside the institutional and policy contexts that generate those outcomes. Moreover, it would have benefited the PPD camp tactically if the mainstream had been forced to spell out their preferred policies to address poverty and redistribution, and their track record of promoting them. This would have made it clear that there had been very little movement on their side, and that the mainstream's interest in distribution remained both secondary and heavily conditional: the exercise was little more than rhetorical and political opportunism. The cost of rhetorical convergence was the capture of the moral and conceptual high ground by the mainstream through their "inclusive growth" (IG) paradigm. However, IG belongs squarely within the (P) WC tradition, and the policy prescriptions associated with it have been successful only exceptionally.

Given this background, DECS and DEPs can be justified in two ways. First, mainstream strategies of growth and development are limited because of their analytical inconsistencies, single-minded focus on capital accumulation and "growth," and—paradoxically, given this obsessive focus—their association with weak macroeconomic performance, growing volatility, recurrent crises, and regressive shifts in the distribution of income, wealth, and power (Alvaredo et al. 2018; Dreher 2006; Fine and Saad-Filho 2014; Jomo and Fine 2006; Milanovic 2016; Palma 1998; Saad-Filho 2011; UNCTAD 2012). Second, despite their considerable value, abstract critiques of the dominant economic paradigm are insufficient; they must be supplemented by alternative macroeconomic strategies in order to counter the argument that neoliberalism is, effectively, "the only game in town" (see, for example, Ghosh 2015). In this context, DECS and DEPs offer a progressive alternative to the mainstream that may find resonance in a large number of countries (UNRISD 2017).

Strategic goals and policy principles

DECS aim to build an inclusive, democratic, diversified, and sustainable economy. This goal can be related to five areas of debate in the fields of economic development, industrial policy, and democratization. They concern (a) poverty, (b) distribution, (c) the environment, (d) policy instruments and goals, and (e) democracy and the protection of identities. These issues are examined in what follows.

First, *mass poverty is an urgent problem especially in the DEs, and it must be addressed by public policy.* [5] For mainstream economics, poverty derives primarily from *exclusion* from market processes because of incomplete markets, market failures, or limitations to voluntary exchange, and it is measured by the inability to reach arbitrary expenditure lines, for example US$1.90, US$5.50 or any other value per day (Dagdeviren et al. 2002). This approach implies that markets are, unproblematically, creators of wealth, and that low incomes are symptomatic of, and due to, exclusion from them. It follows that, for the mainstream, economic growth and poverty reduction ought to be driven by the expansion of markets and the integration of poor people, for example, through new opportunities for paid work, upskilling, or the sale of goods or services (Craig and Porter 2003, 2006).

This is misleading, because it decontextualizes poverty and obscures its sources and structures of reproduction. In minimally complex capitalist economies, poverty can persist because of the lack of markets, jobs, and opportunities for the productive deployment of existing resources (a "Smithian poverty trap"). Alternatively, poverty may be created by the form of integration into the dominant mode of social and economic reproduction (a "Marxian poverty trap"). In the latter case, insufficient income is not merely a symptom of poverty but, rather, one of the implications of the structural inequalities constituting the economic system.

There is no doubt that capitalist forms of economic and social integration can create wealth, for example, by expanding opportunities for market access. However, they can also dispossess the poor, for example, through debt, expulsion from the land due to rural development projects, or the expansion of agribusiness if new roads bring in distant competitors who can dislocate local producers or if new planning laws favor supermarkets at the expense of small shops and street-sellers. Alternatively, capital-intensive technological change can destroy jobs and skills (e.g., through the introduction of tractors, new machines, computers, or robots), deindustrialization can create unemployment, and policy shifts (e.g., trade liberalization or exchange rate policy reforms) can damage small-scale agriculture. Similarly, the self-employed may also find that their economic prospects are depressed because of their insufficient access to credit and markets. Market growth can also create environmental stresses that undermine livelihoods and destroy the productive capabilities of the poor (e.g., rapidly rising commercial demand for fish can lead to overfishing and the collapse of stocks) (Harriss-White 2005).

Economic growth can also impose upon the poor labor regimes associated with low productivity, high exploitation, low incomes, and precarious living standards. These can include badly paid wage labor, child labor, bonded labor, slavery, volatile modalities of market dependence, and insecure and inadequately paid self-employment. The degrading implications of "modern" forms of social reproduction can be aggravated by environmental and other forms of vulnerability, which invariably affect the poor disproportionately (Gunter et al. 2005). It follows that "free markets" do not necessarily or spontaneously eliminate poverty; targeted policies are always needed in order to steer the process of growth toward diversification, resilience, sustainability, social integration, income security, and income redistribution. By the same token, economic concentration tends to increase volatility and enhance the vulnerabilities of the poor.

Mainstream definitions of poverty, limited to the inability to reach an arbitrary level of income, cannot distinguish between Smithian and Marxian poverty-generating processes, and they suggest that "more growth" will always eliminate poverty. Although growth can generate additional resources to support democratic (or any other) outcomes, recognition that growth can *also* generate poverty and inequality suggests that the impact of growth on poverty is maximized, and trade-offs are bypassed, when the process of growth directly addresses both Smithian poverty (conventionally, "the rising tide lifts all boats") and Marxian poverty (which requires policy-steering). By the same token, if the country's mainstream economic strategy fosters stagnation and the reproduction of poverty, targeted social programs and exiguous safety nets may be insufficient to reverse the trend (Saad-Filho 2015).

DECS is informed by a detailed understanding of the structures and processes of economic reproduction and a nuanced assessment of labor and commodity markets, and they recognize that these structures and processes can create *and* eliminate poverty simultaneously. Democratic strategies also recognize that markets and other economic and social structures can be vehicles for the exercise of economic and political power. The elimination of the structures of reproduction of poverty amidst the creation of wealth is primarily a political rather than technical process; in particular, it requires structural reforms to remove the systemic inequalities of access to, and control over, labor, economic resources, and political power.

Second, *democratic development must be equalizing*, that is, *it must benefit the poor more than the rich*. In other words, *growth is democratic only when it reduces both absolute and relative poverty*. Traditionally, growth and equity were perceived to be negatively correlated, at least in the early stages of growth, and this assumption was often used to validate distributionally regressive economic policies (Kuznets 1955). This claim was challenged by empirical evidence suggesting that equality can support rapid economic growth (see, for example, Reinert 2008). At a later stage, the World Bank's IG paradigm suggested that economic growth is almost invariably "good for the poor", because growth almost always alleviates poverty. However, this too easily lends support to misleading policies of "trickle down" and the idea that the distribution of morsels to the desperate can justify the rapid enrichment of the privileged (Cammack 2004; McKinley 2009; Rao 2002). This debate is informative, but DECS bypass it entirely since, in this paradigm, economic policies are *not* selected to maximize growth, equity is *not* an instrument to achieve rapid growth, and there is *no* presumption of a stable trade-off between growth and equity that could be exploited for policy purposes. Instead, in DECS growth must reduce inequalities directly as a condition for democracy (Campos-Vazquez et al. 2017; UNRISD 2012; the importance of social and economic equality is reviewed by Pickett and Wilkinson 2010).

The slow improvement in the welfare of the poor during the last 40 years under neoliberalism is a severe indictment of mainstream economics, the international financial institutions (IFIs), and the so-called "international community," especially in the light of the vast resources available in the world economy and those that could be generated through faster growth, environmental sustainability, and more equitable distribution. Perversely, mainstream policies are not self-correcting, and their failure often leads to the intensification of their preferred economic programs under even closer supervision by the IMF, the World Bank, the US Treasury Department, and many aid agencies. Instead of this doomed path, DECS require

> consistency between the macroeconomic framework and the national poverty reduction strategy. This is usually interpreted as a "one-way" consistency, in which the anti-poverty strategy has to adjust to a fixed and rigid macroeconomic framework. However, both should be jointly determined to serve the overriding objective of poverty reduction.
>
> (UNDP 2002, p. 1)

From a democratic viewpoint, mainstream stabilization and structural adjustment policies centered on price stability and static market-based allocative efficiency are flawed. They tend to focus inordinately on short-term stabilization while, at the same time, undercutting the basis for long-term growth; they worsen the distribution of income and promote environmentally destructive activities. Unsurprisingly, these policies have normally failed to sustain rapid economic growth, create quality jobs, reduce poverty, or support environmental sustainability. In contrast, DECS must include a set of policies establishing a positive feedback loop between growth and distribution, and making distribution essential for growth. *In DECS, distribution is a condition for growth, rather than an incidental outcome*: growth must benefit the poor disproportionately, and it will take place only as long as it does so.

Third, *democratic development must protect the environment*, because humans are not merely part of nature; our numbers, advanced technologies, and environmental footprint have turned our species into stewards of the Earth. DECS recognize the implications of the distinctive position of humanity through the notion of "environmental constraint." This includes each country's control over part of the bounty of nature, the resource needs of production, and the implications of the system of accumulation for the reproduction of life on Earth (Ghosh 2012; Hoffmann 2011; Khor 2011; Storm 2011).

In order to protect nature against the boundless demands of profit extraction, a society infused by ideals of equity, justice, and sustainability should support the gradual autonomization between humans and nature. This can help to overcome the capitalist reliance on the environment as a source of underpriced inputs and as a potential sink for the by-products of accumulation: today, capital profits from the free bounties of nature as it sucks the vitality out of the Earth (UNRISD 2018;

Utting 2015). Shifting the energy matrix from fossil fuels to renewables is a step in this direction; society can also reduce its reliance on other aspects of the environment, for example, fish stocks, endangered rivers and aquifers, marginal agricultural lands, and fragile ecosystems. Instead of the current parasitical relationship with nature, under DECS economic activities (i.e., as the metabolic relationship between society and the rest of nature through which human civilizations reproduce themselves) should seek to build a positive feedback loop between growth, distribution, diversification, and sustainability. This, too, should be a condition for economic growth, rather than an incidental outcome of it.

Fourth, *the goals of DECS—macroeconomic stability, environmental sustainability, and improvements in distribution, social welfare, and economic diversification—should be pursued directly*, rather than being conditional upon trickle down, profit-making, or the interests of finance, and these outcomes must be unambiguous across a broad spectrum of measures. This requires direct changes in the distribution of income and wealth (e.g., through land reform, universal education and training, rising wages and pensions for the poor, and the expansion of entitlements funded by progressive taxation) together with policies promoting economic diversification and environmental protection (e.g., support to strategic sectors, targeted employment generation programs, and regulations to raise productivity and environmental standards) (UNFCCC 2016; UNIDO and GGGI 2015).

Macroeconomic stability includes low inflation, low economic volatility, high rates of employment, rising incomes, intertemporal fiscal and balance of payments equilibrium, and real exchange rate (RER) stability. These desirable outcomes cannot be achieved at the expense of the environment, which must be stable in its own terms; in turn, environmental stability cannot be achieved against the living standards of the poor. *Macroeconomic stability within environmental sustainability* is the best framework for the implementation of democratic economic policies (UNDP 2005). For example, inflation can redistribute income toward finance and the rich, exchange rate volatility can render industries uncompetitive, balance of payments crises can limit essential imports, and unsustainable economic activities damage the planet and can destroy lives and livelihoods now and in the future. In addition, expectations of macroeconomic instability can erode support for the government's democratic policies, undermining their implementation.

In order to minimize the scope for these destabilizing outcomes, the macroeconomic limits of government policy should not be defined precisely in advance. While the democratic policy goals should be described in detail and pursued consistently, the optimal policy stance with respect to the conventional indicators of macroeconomic stability is *constructive ambiguity*. Macroeconomic stability is important because of its instrumental value; however, listing a set of arbitrary restrictions on government action (such as maximum inflation rates or fiscal deficits, or target exchange rates) alongside the strategic aims of DECS undermines their achievement, because it signals that the government is only conditionally committed to the democratic goals. For example, what should the government do if inflation marginally exceeds the target? Which commitments should be prioritized—the maximum inflation rate or the social programs distributing income, providing housing and health, and funding adaptation to climate change? The answer depends on the nature of the imbalances and the political circumstances. This does not imply that macroeconomic stability is unimportant, but recognizes that it has costs; in other words, the preservation of stability should not become a goal in itself, nor should it serve as an excuse to undermine the democratic economic strategy.

Fifth, *democratic economic strategies must be nested within open political processes.* This principle operates at two levels. At the macro level, economic democracy depends on the social and political structures underpinning DECS, especially mass mobilization in support of distribution, diversification, and sustainability (Raworth et al. 2014). Mobilization is essential because democratic policies disconnected from mass protagonism, especially by those with the greatest interest in their success, are populist: they are selected and implemented arbitrarily by political "leaders," making these leaders unaccountable, while those policies remain poorly monitored. These are not merely process failures, but symptoms of political flaws in the strategy itself:

> Political costs (namely, losses for the rich) are usually cited as a rationale for avoiding redistributive policies. We would emphasize, in stark contrast, that the majority of the working population need to mobilize themselves politically so that the "political costs" of not undertaking redistribution become prohibitively high.
> (McKinley 2009, p. 19)[6]

Accountability also increases the resilience of DECS, making them less vulnerable to political shifts either because of changes of government or because of backroom negotiations between the government and the elites. n the absence of transparency, mass intervention, and strong institutions of representation (trade unions, community associations, nongovernmental organizations [NGOs], electoral systems, the Courts, an open media, and so on), it is impossible to gauge support for conflicting goals, select between alternative uses of the available resources, and assess the government's performance.

In turn, at the micro level DECS must protect individual rights and collective identities, including human rights and identities grounded on gender, ethnicity, cultural inheritance, personal choice and lifestyle, and so on. This is not only because of the duty to include everyone as an equal member of society, but also because societies must promote individual flourishing while also recognizing the identities that their members have or choose to partake and their preferred modes of living. Social inclusion, political equality, and the recognition of rights will reinforce policies promoting economic equality and a more harmonious relationship with nature. In contrast, social exclusion, inequality, and alienation from others will foster selfish interests, predatory approaches to the environment, repressive societies, and unsustainable economies.

Principles, policies, and controversies

The policy principles outlined above recognize that state-led coordination of activity is necessary, because the state is a fundamental tool for collective action. The state is the only social institution that is at least potentially democratically accountable,[7] and that can influence the pattern of employment; the production and distribution of goods, services, income, and assets; and the relationship between humans and nature. Only the state can limit the power of selfish interests, raise sufficient funds for democratic economic reforms; and ensure that economic activity is guided by the demands of the majority.

Public institutions play an essential role setting targets, providing integrated planning, coordinating policies, centralizing the allocation of resources, and monitoring performance, in order to address the balance of payments, fiscal, financial, labor, and other constraints (Barrowclough and Kozul-Wright 2018a, 2018b). This approach does not necessarily require political openness, but neither are they mutually incompatible; the construction of democracy is an independent aim rather than an instrumental variable. There are no recipes for that, only principles to be implemented, goals to be agreed, and experiences to be assessed.

In summary, DECS can make an important contribution to the achievement of democratic, distributive, and sustainable economic outcomes, especially in the DEs, where the social needs are greatest. This can be done optimally through a combination of rapid employment-intensive growth, economic diversification, redistribution of income and assets, and implementation of sustainable economic policies. This is not excessively ambitious:

> Very small changes in distribution can have a large effect on poverty head counts ... [For example, if] the share of national income that goes to the poorest population quintile increased from 6 to 6.25 per cent, this would represent a 4 per cent increase in their total income. Thus, a very small redistribution would have the same effect on poverty as doubling the annual growth of national income from 4 per cent ... to 8 per cent ... [Similarly,] over the 15-year forecast period a 5 per cent point change in the Gini makes as much a difference to poverty reduction as an additional 50 per cent growth in consumption per capita. On an annual basis this translates to an additional 1.3 per cent growth per capita.
>
> (Naschold 2004, pp. 108, 118)

Similar principles, grounded in democracy, solidarity, and stewardship of the Earth, also apply internationally. Climate change affects the entire world, albeit in different ways, and only decisive, selfless, and coordinated action can save everyone from the threat of catastrophe (Khor 2011; Millward-Hopkins et al. 2020; Robbins 2020).

Given the principles outlined above, four arguments can be made against DECS. First, some countries are either "too poor to redistribute," or "too poor to mitigate and adapt": their per capita income is so low that redistribution would have little impact on poverty, while environmental sustainability would be too expensive at home and would have an insignificant impact globally. These arguments are invalid: redistribution can have positive outcomes both statically and over time in rich as well as poor countries (Dagdeviren et al. 2002). At the same time, while wealthy countries must bear a larger share of the burden of transition, any contribution will help to achieve global resilience (it remains the case that small and very poor countries should be afforded extra time and resources to adapt).

Second, although redistribution can reduce poverty to some extent, and sustainable policies can ameliorate the impact of climate change, market-based economic growth can deliver both more efficiently; consequently, policymakers should focus on delivering the conditions for growth while leaving growth itself, distribution, and sustainability to the market. This argument is flawed, because untrammelled profit-seeking growth tends to be heavily damaging to the environment; in addition, distribution has tended to deteriorate under neoliberalism

(Cowell and Van Kerm 2015; Dorn and Schinke 2018; Galbraith 2011; Mechling et al. 2017; Onaran and Guschanski 2018; Piketty 2014; UNCTAD 2012). Finally, the uneven track record of several AEs (e.g., the United States, Australia, Canada, and Norway) suggests that high income does not automatically translate into environmentally sustainable policies. More generally, since economic processes always change the technologies of production, patterns of employment, composition of the output, relations of distribution, structures of consumption, and the human impact on the environment, it is appropriate that the economy be subjected to policy influence by democratic means (Cornia and Martorano 2012; Erixon 2018; Saad-Filho 2007).

Third, even if state direction of growth can be effective, it violates democratic principles (Branco 2012; Bruszt 2006; Tomasi 2015; USAID 1998). This argument is otiose. There is a debate about the economic performance of democratic versus authoritarian regimes; for example, it has been claimed that democracy is a "luxury good" that becomes possible only after economic development has already taken place or, alternatively, that authoritarian political systems can deliver growth more efficiently than democracies (Acemoglu and Robinson 2006; Alfano and Baraldi 2016; HDR 2002; Nayyar 2015; Weingast 2015). The controversies around the meaning of democracy, the classification of countries, sample sizes, the timing and significance of political shifts, and so on suggest that the relationship between democracy, growth, and distribution is not clear-cut. In this context, DECS can be justified in two ways. On the one hand, democracy, openness, transparency, accountability of the state, and the representation of conflicting interests are *not* tools for the achievement of economic goals; instead, they are non-negotiable principles of social organization, and any trade-offs are irrelevant. On the other hand, while rapid growth has been achieved in China, Ethiopia, Indonesia, Singapore, South Korea, Taiwan, and elsewhere under authoritarian regimes, experiences in West Germany, Japan, and the Scandinavian countries show that political democracy is compatible with growth, the satisfaction of basic needs, and improvements in distribution. In turn, Bangladesh, Botswana, Brazil, India, Mexico, and other countries present a mixed picture; moreover, there are countless examples of economic failure under democratic as well as under authoritarian regimes, from Nigeria to Venezuela, Myanmar to Italy, and Pakistan to Paraguay. They show that the choice of political regime should be addressed independently from instrumental economic considerations.

Fourth, DECS will be difficult to implement, and several governments have failed in their attempts to follow these types of strategies in the past. This is correct, and there is no guarantee that similar failures will not occur in the future. However, the success stories under democratic as well as authoritarian regimes should also be taken into account, for example in Chile (economic diversification), China (poverty reduction and environmental initiatives), Cuba (policy autonomy and social welfare), India, especially in Kerala State (distribution and welfare), Venezuela (social protection), Vietnam (employment creation and improvements in well-being), and so on.

In summary, the success of DECS depends heavily on the political limitations to implementation. Experience shows that the most important constraint to these strategies, and to economic diversification and environmental sustainability, is not resource scarcity or the balance of payments constraint: it is the lack of political will to do what has become both urgent and imperative for social, political, and environmental reasons. It is essential to confront conventional wisdom and the hegemony of neoliberalism in order to build sustainable alternatives. Experience shows that this is primarily a *political process*, rather than an arena of debate between academic economists. Within these limits, macroeconomic policy can make an important contribution to the complex and contentious process of redressing structural inequalities, eliminating poverty and its symptoms, changing the global energy matrix, restructuring systems of production, and achieving environmental sustainability. The urgency of these challenges, their ramifications, and the difficulty of addressing them while preserving political and economic stability suggest that, unless governments give absolute priority to climate change *and* the satisfaction of basic needs, public policies are likely to achieve neither of these goals. This is the reason for DECS and DEPs.

Notes

1   Emphasis on alternative policies based on the heterodoxy excludes the work of dissenting mainstream economists, such as Jeffrey Sachs and Joseph Stiglitz (for an overview of their recent writings, see http://www.earthinstitute. columbia.edu/about/director/ and http://www0.gsb.columbia.edu/ipd/). Despite their significant contribution at the level of economic policy and their unrivaled capacity to bring to the attention of the media the problems of poverty, environmental degradation, and the limitations of the WC, their critique of mainstream policies remains firmly grounded in neoclassical economics (see Fine et al. 2001; Fine and Van Waeyenberge 2006; Van Waeyenberge 2006).
2   For an overview of the pro-poor policy literature, see Balakrishnan et al. (2010); Cornia (2006); Dagdeviren et al. (2002); Fontana and Sawyer (2016); Kakwani (2001, 2002); Kakwani and Pernia (2000); McCulloch and Baulch

(1999); McKinley (2001, 2003); Osmani (2001); Palanivel (2003); Pasha and Palanivel (2004); Rao (2002); Saad-Filho (2007, 2011); UNDP (2002); Vandemoortele (2004); and Winters (2002).

3 See Ficklin et al. (2018); Gerber and Gerber (2017); Panayotakis (2007); Scales (2014); Storm (2009); and Taylor et al. (2016). Contemporary mainstream strategies of growth and development are outlined by Besley and Cord (2007); CGD (2008); Ostry et al. (2018); and World Bank (2009).

4 In other words, the growth–distribution dichotomy is false, and it is wrong to decompose poverty changes into its growth and distribution components, because the interaction between these elements is not merely additive: the impact of growth on inequality, and the growth-elasticity of poverty, vary with the degree of inequality, the level of development of the country, and so on (see Heltberg 2004).

5 This aim is not only important in itself, it is also mandated by the United Nations through the Universal Declaration of Human Rights (UDHR), the Declaration on the Right to Development (UNDRD), the Millennium Development Goals (MDGs), and the Sustainable Development Goals (SDGs).

6 See also Wiig and Kolstad (2018).

7 This remains true even when states are not democratic in practice, which requires political reforms. In contrast, it is impossible to render for-profit corporations "democratic," since they are accountable to their shareholders and, occasionally (depending on traditions, the law, and the strength of social movements), also to a wider pool of stakeholders, but they are never accountable to society at large.

5 Growth and distribution

This chapter reviews the significance and implications of economic growth in mainstream and heterodox literature, and its relevance for a democratic strategy of economic development. The (in)compatibility between, on the one hand, economic growth and, on the other hand, economic sustainability, especially in view of the challenges of climate change, needs to be addressed in detail. For the mainstream, there is no significant problem, since it is unproblematically assumed that growth can expand the possibilities of consumption, and generate the technologies for climate adaptation. In turn, for sections of the heterodoxy growth must be suspended in order to preserve the environmental balance and avoid a climate catastrophe. This book argues, differently, that economic growth is indispensable for the achievement of global convergence, income growth, and the satisfaction of basic needs in democratic economies and societies, especially in DEs. However, the *type* of growth must be transformed, in order to bring gains to the poor rather than to the rich.

Mainstream views

Between the late 1950s and the early 1970s, the dominant views about the relationship between economic growth, poverty, and inequality tended to draw on the models associated with Kuznets (1955) and Solow (1956). They suggested that the distribution of income tends to deteriorate in the early stages of growth and improve spontaneously later, and that initial per capita income differences between countries would be eroded over time through the equalization of the marginal returns to the factors of production.

In the mid-1970s, many observers concluded that these hopes were misplaced: most poor countries were failing to converge with the rich "core" of the world economy, and the distribution of income was deteriorating in several parts of the world. It was difficult to support the idea that equality-generating processes were gaining strength either in the global economy or within most developing countries. The ensuing debates were, inevitably, framed by the parallel controversies between Keynesians and Monetarists in the Anglo-Saxon AEs. While the Keynesians tended to argue that convergence would require interventionist industrial policies and the redistribution of income, the Monetarists claimed that state intervention would inevitably fail, and that "free market" policies offered the most promising avenue for rapid growth and the improvement of the lot of the poor.

The rise of Monetarism and New Classical Economics between the mid-1970s and the late 1980s shifted the expectations of development theory toward trickle-down, or the spontaneous reallocation of the dividends of growth through the application of economic policies aligned with neoliberalism. The perception that this strategy had failed by the early 1990s, the rise of New Institutional Economics (NIE), and growing pressure on the World Bank and the IMF by several country governments, international organizations (including some UN agencies), NGOs, universities, and social movements compelled the mainstream and the IFIs to address the problems of inequality and poverty reduction explicitly again. During the 1990s and early 2000s, the mainstream approach—now split between the WC and the PWC—was criticized because of its theoretical inconsistencies, responsibility for weak macroeconomic performance and recurrent crises in the poor countries, and regressive shifts in the distribution of power, income, and wealth. For these reasons, the mainstream lost ground to an emerging set of alternatives inspired by democratic values and committed to redistribution.

These shifts became evident in the global commitment to the millennium development goals (MDGs) in 2000 and the sustainable development goals (SDGs) in 2015. However, in the meantime the pendulum swung back again in the mid-2000s in response to a sophisticated attempt by the mainstream to recapture the theoretical, if not moral, high ground through IG. The most significant such attempt was through the World-Bank-sponsored Commission for Growth and Development (CGD 2008).

Despite claims to openness and flexibility, and an abundance of reports purporting to support a new role for public policy, the IFIs invariably advance a detailed list of "correct" economic policies for all countries. The argument normally starts from a standard list of ambitions, including a stable macroeconomic environment; fiscal responsibility; price stability; improving the investment climate; strengthening property rights; regulatory improvements to reduce transaction costs; high savings and investment rates; transparent markets responsible for resource allocation; greater access to infrastructure; improved mobility of resources, especially labor; trade openness and strategic integration with the world economy; and a capable, credible, and effective government committed to growth. Distributive concerns are noticeably absent, except insofar as inequality might trigger political unrest,[1] or hamper the translation of growth into absolute poverty reduction (Besley and Cord 2007). Aside from these reservations, the IFIs and mainstream economists focus almost entirely on the importance of growth to reduce absolute poverty, while they bypass distributional policies entirely (see Chapter 4).

From this point of view, growth requires—in addition to the above list—a competitive environment; a government commitment to growth (rather than simply the absence of government); public sector investment in infrastructure and in physical and human capital; deregulation of the labor market; rising productivity growth; international integration; exchange rate management in order to maintain export competitiveness; and the liberalization of international capital flows in order to lower the cost of capital. However, liberalization should be gradual both because foreign savings are an imperfect substitute for domestic savings, and because excessively rapid liberalization introduces avoidable risks (CGD 2008). Capital controls should be imposed if necessary.[2] Finally, social safety nets can "provide a source of income to people between jobs—and ensure uninterrupted access to basic services ... Without them, popular support for a growth strategy will quickly erode (CGD 2008, p. 6).

In summary, for the mainstream the welfare impact of growth derives primarily from faster growth itself (through trickle down, employment gains, higher tax revenues, and so on) rather than, say, from policies targeting directly the constraints faced by the poor (Besley and Cord 2007). The World Bank has expressed high hopes that this approach would be successful: "There are important lessons to learn from this approach including that development policy is country-specific, may involve just a few reforms that can be optimally sequenced to relax binding constraints, and it may lead to large positive welfare impacts" (World Bank 2009, p. 9). However, experience with (P)WC policies shows that markets are not efficient in the abstract, and they cannot provide the parameters to assess economic efficiency in general. Conventional perceptions of market efficiency are normally based on an idealization of what the financial or currency markets do, as opposed to, say, the markets for oil, healthcare, or automobiles, which operate in profoundly distinct ways and where efficiency is assessed very differently.

The importance of growth

The ambiguous and potentially shifting relationships between economic growth, on the one hand, and, on the other hand, diversification, technology, inequality, poverty, and the environment (see Chapter 4), carry four implications. First, economic growth causes global warming, and the replication of the patterns of consumption of the rich around the world, with current technologies or those that can be developed in the time available, will lead to the collapse of the Earth's environment. Nevertheless, growth can *also* generate resources and new technologies for resilience and adaptation (Ackerman et al. 2012; Thompson 2020; Wiedman et al. 2020).

Second, in order to maximize the distributive and poverty-alleviating impact of growth, and to generate resources and technologies for redistribution, social protection, mitigation, and adaptation to climate change, the rates of investment and growth in DEs must be high (UNIDO 2015)—that is, DECS require "bolder and more expansionary" policies than those that are possible under mainstream development strategies (McKinley 2004, p. 1). Faster growth can also increase economic resilience through investments in productive assets, diversification, and employment creation (Dercon 2014; Hoffmann 2015; Lohmann 2009; UNDESA 2013). In turn, distributive policies must be coordinated with the expansion of the economy to generate the necessary funding, reduce volatility, minimize the scope for poverty-creating growth trajectories, iron out potential labor scarcities or gluts (e.g., engineers driving taxis or nurses selling food in kiosks), and address the poverty-generating implications of climate change, which weigh heavily upon those who are already disadvantaged.

Third, investment and growth must be targeted around diversification, the needs of the poor, and the environmental constraint. Key sectors are likely to include those that generate income and employment for the poor, upskill participants in the labor markets, and produce (mostly labor-intensive and non-tradable) goods and services consumed by the poor. Examples include small-scale agriculture, construction, repair workshops, and services industries processing food and industrial inputs. Public works programs can relieve supply constraints, for example through the construction of roads and irrigation facilities. In most DEs, it will also be important to support the development of agriculture and its linkages with other economic sectors, both because of their economic importance and because of the fact that large numbers of poor people live in rural areas.

Fourth, these efforts, in the scale required and in the time available, especially in the poor countries, require a focus on infrastructure, including roads, ports, and airports in priority areas; telecommunications; renewable electricity generation and new transmission lines; greening production chains; retrofitting the building stock; expanding the provision of housing, water, sewerage, public transport and health; sustainable irrigation facilities; and education and technical training compatible with the demands of the new democratic economy (Sekar et al. 2019b; Sinclair-Desgagné 2013).[3] These initiatives can be successful only with state planning, regulation, funding, and performance assessments. In doing this, DEs can draw upon successful experiences in Chile, China, South Korea, and Indonesia between the 1970s and the 1990s, and those in China, Ethiopia, Malaysia, and Vietnam subsequently. The mere manipulation of interest rates, which is the focus of neoliberal "horizontal" economic policies, is insufficient to induce and direct investment and growth, or to achieve the wider goals of democratic development.

The mainstream expectation that economic growth is a panacea is misplaced. Even when mainstream strategies are successful, they tend to induce economic growth centered on traditional comparative advantages. They also feed economic concentration, damage the environment, and neglect or even enhance structural inequalities that create poverty even as the economy expands. If income and productivity growth are sufficiently rapid, most people benefit even if inequality grows (e.g., Brazil and Mexico between the 1950s and the 1970s, the Gulf economies between the early 1970s and the mid-1980s, and China since the 1980s). However, if GDP growth is low or erratic, it can lead to the decline of the living standards of large numbers of people (e.g., Russia and other former soviet countries since the early 1990s, and most Middle Eastern, African, and poor Latin American countries between the early 1980s and the late 1990s). In addition, growth can have environmental implications that may not be readily identifiable and cannot be attributed precisely, but that will impose costs on livelihoods and on the planet itself.

The DEs have pressing needs for economic growth and structural change. If the world is to become more equal, these countries must upgrade their technological and productive capabilities. They can achieve income and productivity gains in two principal ways. One is through mass production facilities where low-paid unskilled workers engage in repetitive tasks at high speed—for example, in traditional plantations or in manufacturing industries producing clothing, shoes, or standard electronic products, as in Mexico's *maquiladoras* or in many Asian export processing zones. Alternatively, relatively well-paid skilled workers can apply more sophisticated technical skills and advanced machinery in the production of non-traditional electronic and capital goods, chemicals, and specialist agricultural commodities, or in the services sector. Both avenues offer important advantages, but most DEs would find it difficult to internalize advanced production techniques rapidly because they lack the managerial capacity, skills, finance, technology, and infrastructure to do so.

In spite of these limitations, DECS should aim to incorporate, at least in the medium term, and in selected areas, aspects of the "high road" to development outlined above. The "high road" offers several advantages. It opens new export opportunities in expanding economic sectors, which can help to relieve the balance of payments constraint and diversify oil-dependent economies. It requires the development of chains of related activities that will expand growth and employment in other areas of the economy. It demands a skilled workforce, which will transfer their expertise to other sectors when they change jobs or if they open small businesses. These workers will be better paid than the average, which will raise the aspirations of workers employed elsewhere. Finally, more productive firms can set high standards of workplace safety and security that will facilitate the regulation and eventually the elimination of unsafe and degrading working conditions in other sectors.

High productivity gives firms the scope to grow, diversify, and improve pay and conditions, rather than impose wage cuts, shed labor whenever they are hit by demand pressures, or adopt damaging technologies from the point of view of the environment simply because they are cheaper for the individual business. "The market" does not always spontaneously generate new exports, internalize value chains, adopt sustainable development strategies, reduce carbon emissions, pay salaries commensurate with productivity, deliver adequate health and safety standards in the workplace, or support the diffusion of technologies compatible with the stabilization of the Earth's climate (Kemp and Never 2017). State regulation, incentives, international agreements, and trade union intervention are essential to achieve these outcomes. Diversification, mitigation, productivity growth, higher salaries, and improved working conditions can also be promoted by legislation offering tax and other incentives for firms investing in priority sectors, adopting sustainable output mixes, technologies, and business models, and paying high wages. These policies can be partly funded by progressive (national as well as global) taxes, fees, and contributions (see Chapter 7).

Gradual and steady wage growth while reducing wage dispersion will benefit not only the low-paid workers but also the most productive firms, especially in capital-intensive sectors. These firms will capture extraordinary profits not only through higher productivity but also through the expansion of the domestic market, while less efficient firms will face losses. Export incentives, targeted credit, and import protection (to the maximum extent permitted by WTO rules and the relevant trade agreements) will support the adjustment of the labor-intensive sectors to the new policy regime while offering an alternative avenue for profitability and growth. Finally, the workers left unemployed because of the bankruptcy of the inefficient firms or the declining availability of low-paid jobs should be retrained with public funds in order to find more productive and better-paying employment elsewhere. These medium-term policies will help to raise productivity, increase labor market flexibility, and reduce structural unemployment while creating incentives for exports and long-term productivity growth.

High levels of employment and high wages are essential for the improvement of the welfare of the majority. This will require negotiations around desirable outcomes in terms of wage increases, productivity growth, and economic stability. The experience of Scandinavian countries, Austria, and Australia can offer useful pointers for achieving these outcomes. In these negotiations, regulation, credit, export, and employment incentives, import policies, and other forms of public sector intervention can promote democratic outcomes. Obviously, economic growth creates environmental stresses that can trigger climate change, and high growth rates are necessary but insufficient to address the balance of payments constraint. This leads to three important conclusions directly following from the analysis in this chapter.

First, rapid economic growth can destroy the environment, but it can also generate resources and technologies for climate mitigation and adaptation (Turner 2020a); growth can also support welfare improvements directly by expanding the size of the "cake" and, indirectly, by allowing everyone to see improvements in their own standard of living even if they lose out in relative terms because of shifts in distribution. Redistribution is much harder in stagnant economies, where some groups must suffer losses so that others may gain.

Second, the state plays an essential role in coordinating growth, investment, and distribution. DECS require a close articulation between private and public sector activities, and the regulation of intersectoral and intertemporal resource allocation (including international capital flows) through industrial and financial policy (see above).

Third, for the reasons listed above economic growth is important for the DEs, making strategies of "zero growth" or "degrowth" (Demaria et al. 2013; Germain 2017; Kallis et al. 2012; see also Rezai and Stagl 2016) economically unjustifiable and politically indefensible outside the Global North. The idea that climate change demands economic stasis is utopian under capitalism and, lacking the impulse for systemic change, it is also a recipe for hopelessness and for the marginalization of progressive forces in the most populous, fastest-growing, most imbalanced, and most poverty-stricken regions in the world. It would be more realistic and attractive to campaign for *fast and targeted growth* focusing on improvements in welfare (since the needs of the poor cannot be legitimately deferred), distribution (since the poor are many but, individually, they create less environmental stresses than the rich), climate change mitigation and adaptation (because of the threat of catastrophe), and diversification through green technologies (as the only way to reduce the destructive impact of humans on Earth). This program ought to be coupled with a strong retrenchment of consumption by the rich, both as the lowest "hanging fruit" available to facilitate cuts in CO_2 emissions, and to finance the investments required to protect life on this planet.

Notes

1 In particular, the CGD (2008, p. 7) expressed concerns that Kuznets-type inequality might trigger political instability: 'in the early stages of growth, there is a natural tendency for income gaps to widen. Governments should seek to contain this inequality … Otherwise, the economy's progress may be jeopardized by divisive politics, protest, and even violent conflict'.
2 "Yes, capital controls are leaky, but so are taxes, and that does not stop governments from trying to tax their citizens" (Kuczynski, quoted in CGD 2008, p. 52).
3 These examples are merely indicative. The impact of growth on poverty depends on the initial distribution of income and, especially, its distribution near the poverty line, as well as the occupational composition, skills and other features of the workforce.

6 Democratic policies for diversification, distribution, and development

This chapter focuses on the potential role, choice, and implementation of DECS to drive economic growth, diversification, distribution, and welfare gains, and to create a sustainable future. The chapter examines, in sequence, fiscal, monetary, and financial policies; the role of public investment; the balance of payments constraint; and social policies and equity. These policies can help to address the urgent challenges imposed by climate change, especially in the DEs, but with wider applicability, as they draw upon a large number of successful experiences of development.

Fiscal, monetary, and financial policies

Fiscal (that is, tax-and-spend) policy uses public sector institutions to target social resources (taxes, primary commodity rents, gains from trade, productivity gains, and so on) in priority sectors. Experience shows that fiscal policy can support economic diversification, secure macroeconomic stability, manage aggregate demand, promote productivity growth and environmental sustainability, and relax the supply constraints to growth. Fiscal policy can also help to sustain business confidence and consumer expectations at a time of uncertainty in the world economy both in the short term (for example, due to the coronavirus pandemic in 2020, or in times of financial instability and protectionist pressures) and in the long term (given the implications of climate change). In doing this, fiscal policy can play an essential role in the reduction of poverty and the improvement of the welfare of the majority (Anderson et al. 2016; UNCTAD 2019). This is especially important in poor and middle-income countries with concentrated economic structures, which tend to suffer greater volatility and more severe and frequent economic crises than the AEs, and which will suffer heavily from climate change (see Chapter 3).

Despite its potential significance, fiscal policy has been downgraded under neoliberalism, just as economies tended to become financialized; in the meantime, monetary and financial policies have gained prominence (Saad-Filho 2018). Monetary and financial policies refer to the level of interest rates and, at a further remove, the regulations on banking, credit, and capital flows. The key difference between them is that, while fiscal policies are "vertical" and use the power of the state to direct resources according to the priorities of public policy (some of which may conflict with the short-term interests of the financial sector), monetary and financial policies are "horizontal," that is, they do not distinguish between economic sectors. Instead, shifts in interest rates, bank reserves, and capital flows aim to stabilize inflation, improve expectations, and boost asset prices *in general*. These are priorities for the financial institutions, which control the allocation of resources under neoliberalism. In summary, DECS require restoring the primacy of fiscal policy and "vertical" industrial policies while, also, preserving monetary policy autonomy (that is, the ability to set the variables of monetary policy independently), which is severely curtailed by the liberalization of finance and international capital flows.

In most countries, especially resource-rich DEs, the fiscal policies supporting DECS will become viable only if the tax system is modernized and the tax base is expanded and made more progressive (Ossowski and Halland 2019). It is simply impossible to finance the necessary initiatives with tax rates often lower than 20 percent of GDP, as is common in the Global South, or with regressive taxation, which has been the tendency under neoliberalism.[1] This will require stricter tax laws and the reduction of deductions, exemptions, and loopholes favoring large corporations and the well-off. It will also be necessary to raise tax rates for the rich, and tax wealth, large and second properties, unearned income, capital gains, financial transactions, and "environmental sins", focusing on CO2e emissions at all points along the chains of production and consumption.[2] At the same time, the poor should be protected through tax rebates, credits, and transfers (ETC 2018; IMF 2019; Schwerhoff et al. 2020). In very poor countries, the fiscal resources available may be insufficient to fund diversification and democratic goals (World Bank 2018). In this case, DECS may need to be supplemented by global taxes, aid, other unrequited transfers, and debt forgiveness.

The argument above implies a rejection of financial liberalization and so-called "market-based" (i.e., US- or UK-style) financial systems, which promote "arms-length" relationships between banks and the corporate sector (Zysman 1983). This type of relationship is destabilizing, because it fosters short-termist and self-interested behavior. For example, when firms are doing well, they display no loyalty toward their banks and, conversely, during a crisis the banks tend to cut their losses and deny credit to firms, propagating bankruptcies and unemployment. This is undesirable for a democratic economic strategy. In addition, financial liberalization has generally failed to raise savings, investment, the quality of investment, and the GDP growth rate, and it has frequently worsened the distribution of income (Bumann and Lensink 2013; Hamdaoui and Maktouf 2019; Palma 1998; Studart 2005). Financial liberalization also raises interest rates and feeds bouts of speculation with foreign assets, builds up external and domestic debt, and generates recurring threats of economic collapse if government policies diverge from the interests of the financial institutions (Jalilian and Kirkpatrick 2005).[3]

The weight and influence of the financial sector, its inbuilt short-termism, and the destabilizing impact of financial crises make it essential to regulate finance in order to align its operations with the priorities of DECS and to fund diversification, sustainability, and distribution. These regulations are relevant regardless of the ownership structure of the financial institutions (e.g., whether they are state-owned or privately owned). In general, the achievement of the strategic goals of DECS will be limited if the financial system is excessively concentrated or internationalized, if credit remains scarce except for the elite, and if the financial institutions tend to concentrate their assets in liquid papers, consumer loans, and financial speculation.

Instead of unstable market-based relationships, DECS require close links between firms and banks that are mediated by public policy rather than by the capital markets. This can be partly addressed by large and efficient state-owned and development banks, which are not driven by short-term profit maximization. These banks can introduce competitive pricing practices into the financial markets, and limit the bias of large and transnational banks toward high-value speculative transactions that bring little benefit to the poor. State-owned and development banks can more easily implement anticyclical policies, such as building up reserves in good times and lending in difficult times, and their weight will make it easier to direct credit toward socially desirable goals, including strategic industries, employment-generating small and medium enterprises, and infrastructure. These uses of funds can provide significant positive externalities, but they tend to be ignored by private financial institutions. This arrangement can better support the priorities of DECS, including industrial policy, regional development, economic diversification, environmental sustainability, and redistribution. This type of financial structure can find inspiration in the examples of Germany, Japan, South Korea, and Taiwan during their periods of accelerated growth (Amsden 2001; Reinert et al. 2018).

Finally, fashionable suggestions that poor countries should prioritize microcredit and microfinance initiatives should be rejected (see Bateman 2010, 2014; and Bateman et al. 2018). On the one hand, there is no evidence that any number of anecdotes of success adds up to economic development or sustainability, much less to meaningful investment in strategic sectors. On the other hand, experience shows that microfinance uses scarce savings to support the informalization of production and the dismantling of the labor markets. In doing this, it leads to the haphazard proliferation of low productivity activities, for example street trading, petty food sales, kiosks, and subsistence production. Their funding through microfinance crowds out larger-scale projects that could support quality jobs, productivity-enhancing technologies, diversification, backward and forward linkages, and environmental sustainability. Consequently, even though microfinance can bring short-term benefits to some of the poor, it fosters a macroeconomic spiral of fragmentation of systems of provision, productivity decline, and concentration of resources on trade instead of production that cannot contribute to environmental sustainability, sustained growth, or the development of new competitive advantages. These outcomes are incompatible with DECS.

Investment

It is well known that investment is the driving force of growth; at the same time, growth is the driving force of investment because rapid and sustained growth generates the demand that makes individual investment projects viable with the least compression of disposable incomes, moderating the political and distributive tensions due to economic restructuring.[4] In order to kick-start the virtuous circle of investment, growth, technological improvement, demand growth, greater equality, balance of payments sustainability, and (where necessary) economic diversification, it is necessary to identify the sectors and initiatives that can drive each of these aspects of DECS. Their expansion should be fostered through targeted (vertical) industrial policies, public investment, and focused incentives for the expansion of capacity and output:

> The concept of "focused" incentives excludes the traditional sort of broad investment incentives often employed by governments— tax holidays for investments of any type or general protections from foreign competition. In shaping an alternative economic

development strategy, a government does not simply want more investment; it wants more investment of a certain kind. This requires that incentives be focused.

(MacEwan 2003)

Targeted investments, especially those led by the public sector, can achieve several goals simultaneously (Vercelli 2017). They can increase the supply of strategically important goods and services, support environmental programs, fund diversification, boost new industries, create good jobs in priority areas, alleviate the balance of payments constraint, enlarge the possibilities of consumption, and reduce poverty, especially in economies operating below potential (Hoexter 2014). Public sector investment provides the critical link between short-term stabilization and long-term outcomes. In the absence of targeted investment and rapid growth mediated by accommodating fiscal, monetary and financial policies (if necessary, backed up by foreign transfers, including aid and debt forgiveness), diversification and the build-up of resilience against climate change will be hampered and poverty-reducing outcomes would become dependent on redistribution, which can intensify political stresses.

Although mainstream economics generally insists that public investment both crowds out and is less efficient than private investment, empirical studies offer no clear evidence for this claim. Quite the contrary: public investment can *crowd in* investments in upstream and downstream sectors such as those supplying inputs and consumables, cleaning, maintenance and security services, trading and finance, workforce training, and so on (Berg et al. 2015; Bloch et al. 2016; Fournier 2016; Fournier and Johansson 2016; Johansson 2016; Saia et al. 2015; Slemrod 2015; Warner 2014; for a significant turnaround, see IMF 2005). Public investment can also support private investment and output growth when it expands physical infrastructure, boosts labor productivity, and fosters private savings. Infrastructure is especially important, because it tends to draw on domestic resources (i.e., it generates minimum balance of payments pressures for the additional GDP growth). Infrastructure growth—especially if it is connected to regional integration projects—can improve the living standards of the poor and support the expansion of production across several sectors, with a regionally differentiated impact. The distributive implications of this modality of growth can be maximized if it draws upon public works programs and is combined with the expansion of public pensions and other transfers. Historical evidence shows, first, that public investment has played an essential role in fostering growth and reducing poverty in several dynamic economies in East Asia, Latin America, and elsewhere, and, second, that when public investment falters aggregate profits decline, reducing the incentives (and the resources available) for private investment. Finally, public investment can also support quality foreign investment and improvements in technology and sustainability.

Rather than allocating investments on the basis of "blind" and selfish financial market structures and processes, choices between alternative goals and their resourcing needs should recognize competing interests, and seek to build social cohesion around the core values of democracy, sustainability, stewardship of nature, and responsibility for future generations.[5] The inevitable debates about competing priorities can be informed by a "democratic rate of return," which would help to decide between projects ranked according to their impact on welfare, livelihoods, and democratic rights, and on the basis of their financial feasibility, ecological sustainability, externalities, and support for diversification. In order to qualify, projects should normally yield positive net present values, but there is no need to select those yielding maximum profits, especially if these (as is usual) do not incorporate social and environmental externalities.[6]

Balance of payments and exchange rate policy

The currencies of most countries are not international means of circulation or reserve value. These limitations impose on them a balance of payments constraint, which is probably 'the single most important constraint on capital accumulation and growth' (UNCTAD 2002, p. 32). The balance of payments can trigger exchange rate crises, inflation, unemployment, and other destabilizing processes, with severe consequences for the poor. The AEs generally have a looser balance of payments constraint than the DEs, and their supply bottlenecks can usually be bypassed through imports funded in their own currency or by foreign currency attracted by interest rate movements or marginal regulatory changes.

The balance of payments constraint includes two types of restrictions, on trade (the current account) and on capital flows (the capital and financial account). Mainstream economic strategies invariably recommend the liberalization of imports in order to foster competition and productivity growth, and to shift resources toward the economy's (presumably given) comparative advantages. These policies are not conducive to diversification, the development of new production capabilities, productivity growth, macroeconomic stability, sustainability, mitigation of climate change, or improvements in distribution and the welfare of the poor. Instead, trade and financial policies should be part of an integrated DECS, with four key aspects.

The first aspect is the promotion and diversification of exports, subject to the restriction that *global* carbon emissions must decline. Once this condition is satisfied, exports can play an essential role in the generation of trade surpluses and the accumulation of currency reserves, which are important to minimize balance of payments vulnerability, macroeconomic volatility, and exchange rate fluctuations. In the absence of sizable currency reserves obtained through trade surpluses, DEs would have to seek, at least periodically, more volatile forms of international finance (especially short-term loans and portfolio capital inflows) or borrow from the IFIs, whose conditionalities would limit their ability to pursue democratic policies. Exports can also contribute to productivity growth, because they expose local producers to the test of competition in foreign markets.

Export growth requires a competitive and stable real exchange rate (see below), as well as coordinated industrial policy initiatives to develop the country's competitive advantages in strategically important sectors and to promote new, green, and export-capable industries. These priority areas require government involvement in the task of "picking winners" and supporting their expansion, which has been addressed successfully by several East Asian and Latin American countries and, most recently, by China (Amsden 1997, 2001; Chang and Grabel 2004; Reinert et al. 2018; the benefits of trade diversification for growth are reviewed by Keen 2017 and Lederman and Maloney 2012). Their experiences can inform policies fostering the creation, nurturing, and growth of firms tasked with delivering export growth, as well as distributional improvements, diversification, and sustainability. It goes without saying that these initiatives should avoid tilting incentives excessively toward tradables. Although sustained income growth requires the expansion of the tradables sector, non-tradables are also important because they have a large employment-generating potential and tend to employ technologies that are generally simpler and less intensive in foreign resources. Countries should also be aware that gains from trade can be concentrated in sectors that are competitive only in the short term, or in environmentally destructive enclaves, or sectors offering high returns for skills or assets that are socially undesirable, unsustainable, or beyond the reach of the poor. This would tend to increase the inequalities of income and wealth, locking the economy into an undesirable position from a democratic and egalitarian point of view and, possibly, accelerating climate change.

The second aspect is the management of the country's import restrictions. Despite mainstream claims to the contrary, "openness and trade integration, either separately or together, do *not* have a measurable impact on long-run growth" (Weller and Hersh 2004, p. 492; see also Abbas 2014). Imports should be liberalized cautiously and selectively because of their potentially adverse impact on the poor, existing inequalities, environmental sustainability, carbon emissions, and strategic sectors (Harrison et al. 2011; ITF 2015; Le Goff and Singh 2013; Siddiqui 2015). Trade selectivity is further complicated in oil-export-dependent poor countries that tend to rely on large volumes of imported goods that cannot immediately be competed away. Import liberalization can also increase predatory competition, reducing economic growth and the wages and the employment opportunities of the poor. Finally, subsidized exports from the rich countries (e.g., grains, sugar, cotton, fruit, meat, dairy products, and so on) can undermine the viability of small-scale agriculture and the livelihoods of millions of rural poor, or promote patterns of consumption incompatible with environmental stability. In sum:

> [I]t is incorrect to assume that trade liberalisation will automatically yield outcomes that are pro-poor, pro-jobs and pro-growth ... *[O]pen trade is more a result of development rather than a prerequisite for it.* As countries grow richer, they gradually take advantage of new opportunities offered by global trade. Trade follows development; it seldom leads development.
>
> (Vandemoortele 2004, p. 14, emphasis added)

In a similar vein, in their pioneering study of openness Weller and Hersh conclude that

> the income shares of the poor are lower in countries with deregulated current and capital accounts compared to more regulated ones. This is not because trade is directly harmful for the poor but because of the institutional design under which trade is conducted ... [T]he short-term adverse effects of current and capital account deregulation on the income shares of the poor are not offset by faster income growth in the long-run ... [because] liberalization has no robust impact on growth rates. But ... trade may have a beneficial effect on the income shares of the poor in the short-run in a regulated environment ... [In sum,] countries where trade and capital flows [are] regulated ... do best for the poor.
>
> (Weller and Hersh 2004, pp. 499–500)

The third aspect is that economic diversification in general, and DECS specifically, require the regulation of the capital and financial account of the balance of payments as well as capital controls to curb outflows in pursuit of easy profits. Unregulated capital movements can foster the accumulation of foreign debt, promote speculative inflows to finance unsustainable patterns of production and consumption, facilitate capital flight, misalign the RER, and increase the country's vulnerability to balance of payments crises:

> [T]he boom-bust cycles associated with rapid entry and exit of capital under open capital account regimes tend to deepen poverty not only by undermining investment and growth, but also by leading to regressive income distribution. Surges in capital inflows often lead to a deviation of key macroeconomic aggregates such as savings, investment, fiscal and external balances, exchange rates, employment and wages from their longer-term, sustainable levels. The rapid exit of capital and financial crises, on the other hand, tend to lead to overshooting in the opposite direction. The recovery process, which restores aggregate income to pre-crisis levels, generally results in a different configuration of key macroeconomic variables from those previously prevailing, often resulting in large shifts in income distribution and heightened poverty, which can be corrected only after many years of growth ... Reduced incomes and employment in organized and informal labour markets are the main social conduit of the adverse impact of financial crises on poverty and equality.
>
> (UNCTAD 2002, p. 33)[7]

Capital controls are also needed to protect monetary policy autonomy, and to allow the state to direct investment and other resource flows to growth-promoting, poverty-reducing, and environmentally sustainable goals, which may conflict with the short-term interests of the financial sector. These goals can be assisted by the devaluation of the currency and by the judicious use of currency reserves and sovereign wealth funds to offset the macroeconomic impact of the inflow of real resources.[8] Finally, capital controls can help to curb tax evasion, since the tax rates required to fund diversification and distributive and sustainable goals will almost inevitably be higher than abroad. The adverse implications of capital account liberalization are especially damaging for the poor:

> The link between capital flows and incomes of the poor arises from a greater probability of financial crises in a liberalized environment. More capital flows, especially short-term portfolio flows, are often associated with a greater chance of financial crises ... [T]he

burdens of financial crisis are disproportionately borne by a country's poor ... Although high-income earners are more likely to hold financial assets and hence to be hurt by a crisis through declining asset values, low-income earners may be more likely to be affected by declining demand as unemployment rises ... The poor are the first to lose under such fiscal contractions, and the last to gain when crises subside and fiscal spending expands.

(Weller and Hersh 2004, pp. 478–479)

Several modalities of control over speculative and short-termist movements of capital have been used in Brazil, Chile, China, Japan, Malaysia, South Korea, Sweden, and elsewhere (Alami 2020; Bush 2019; Chang and Grabel 2004; Cozzi and Nissanke 2009; Eichengreen and Rose 2014; Epstein 2005; Grabel 2004; Versteeg 2008). In these countries,

[t]he use of controls has not resulted in interruptions of economic growth; on the contrary, when controls have been removed, as in Mexico in the early 1990s and in East Asia in the late 1990s, financial crises and severe economic downturns have been the result ... Whatever form they take, *controls over the movement of funds across a country's borders are a necessary part of any general program of economic change*; without such controls, a government cedes the regulation of its economy to international market forces, which often means the forces of large internationally operating firms and powerful governments of other countries.

(MacEwan 2003, p. 6)

Capital controls can include restrictions on foreign currency bank accounts and on currency transfers; taxes or administrative limits on outflows of direct and portfolio investment; restrictions on foreign payments for "technical assistance" between connected firms; non-interest-bearing "quarantines" on investment inflows; controls on foreign borrowing; and multiple exchange rates determined by the priority of each type of investment. Managing these controls will burden the monetary authorities, but experience shows that this task is not beyond the capabilities of most central banks, which already regulate domestic finance and oversee international payments as a matter of course. In other words, the most significant obstacle to capital controls is not technical: it is political.

Finally, a DECS-compatible exchange rate regime can choose between full dollarization (or euroization, etc.), fixed or adjustable exchange rates, managed floating with routine interventions, or free-floating regimes (which are too unstable to be considered seriously especially by DEs). Dollarization is the most constraining system (Ecuador, El Salvador, Zimbabwe), and it should be avoided wherever possible. In turn, small countries with extensive currency substitution may have to adopt fixed exchange rate systems (Bosnia and Herzegovina, Iraq, Jordan, United Arab Emirates). This is not ideal, because the need to defend the exchange rate inevitably constrains fiscal and monetary policies, but it may be unavoidable in the short term. In this case, fiscal policies become even more important (see above). Other countries may be able to adopt a managed floating exchange rate regime (Argentina, Brazil, South Africa, Zambia) or, even better, an adjustable peg (China), which maximizes the scope for policy discretion. Whatever the exchange rate regime, it must be managed carefully. Although overvaluation can offer immediate benefits through cheaper imports and lower inflation, DECS should avoid this type of "exchange rate populism": overvaluation can be destructive for domestic production and employment, and it can induce consumption and asset bubbles that may be difficult to neutralize. Experience suggests that economic diversification and the growth of productivity, exports, and employment are more easily obtained with selective import restrictions, export incentives, capital controls, and a moderately undervalued exchange rate (Agosín and Tussie 1993; Gereffi and Wyman 1990; Leibovici and Crews 2018; Lukauskas et al. 2013; Rajagopal 2018). This may be achieved in different ways, including a relatively low peg; expansionary monetary policies; the regulation of currency trading; capital controls; and regular interventions in the currency markets.

Social policies

Mainstream economists generally claim that market processes, "trickle-down," and targeted social programs can secure full employment, distribute productivity gains fairly, eradicate extreme poverty, eliminate inequalities grounded in non-economic factors (Lazear 2000), and deliver sustainability. In reality, however, social policies under neoliberalism tend to be insufficient at the best of times, since they focus on the *management* of the poverty and deprivation created by the system of accumulation itself, rather than on the elimination of poverty and the achievement of social and environmental sustainability. They are also easily overwhelmed by economic fluctuations and crashes: if the country's macroeconomic strategy fosters stagnation and the reproduction of poverty, targeted social programs and exiguous safety nets are insufficient to reverse the trend (Kidd 2017).

Neoliberal social policies are typically targeted and conditional, but this approach is limited for several reasons: these policies tend to be relatively expensive to run, miss out many potential claimants, are prone to corruption, and allocation is always arbitrary at the margin (Saad-Filho 2015). Vandemoortele rightly notes that:

> [n]arrowly targeted programmes are increasingly prescribed for reasons of efficiency and cost savings—for they claim to minimise leakage to the non-poor ... As far as basic services are concerned, narrow targeting can have huge hidden costs ... [because] it is often difficult to identify the poor and to reach them because the non-poor ... seldom fail to capture a large part of subsidies destined for more destitute people. Also, administering narrowly targeted programmes is at least twice as costly as running untargeted ones. In addition, the poor must frequently document eligibility – which involves expenses such as bus fares, apart from the social stigma they generate ... Most importantly, however, is the fact that once the non-poor cease to have a stake in narrowly targeted programmes, the political commitment to sustain their scope and quality is at risk. The voice of the poor alone is usually too weak to maintain strong public support.
>
> Vandemoortele (2004, p. 12)

Transfers also tend to be insufficient to dent poverty when the distribution of income and assets is highly unequal. In these circumstances, more ambitious policy reforms, including the distribution of assets, become essential.

Democratic economic strategies have a much more ambitious and transformative agenda: they seek to build inclusive societies and diversified and sustainable economies. This requires policies to improve living standards, expand welfare provision, protect the poor, reduce inequalities across multiple dimensions (e.g., employment, gender, region, and ethnic background), and build a culture based on citizenship, solidarity, and mutual respect. In order to maximize their impact, democratic social programs should focus on universal policies (available to all on the basis of their belonging to society, regardless of profession, income, citizenship status or any other condition). These policies tend to have the largest distributional impact and minimum managerial costs, and they improve the standard of living of the poor directly (Lawson et al. 2019; Leubolt et al. 2013; Saad-Filho 2007, 2015). They include the provision of public goods and services (the social wage), for example, public education, training, health, housing, transportation, water and sanitation, food security, clothes and shoes, parks and public amenities, and environmental preservation:

> These programs meet people's basic needs, contributing to the reduction of poverty and to the equalization of the income distribution; they thus generate immediate benefits. Many of these programs ... contribute to people's productivity, laying a foundation for more successful, long-term economic expansion. The production process to create and operate social programs is often labor intensive, and thus their implementation tends to use the resource most abundant in low and middle income countries and ... tends to be employment-creating ... Often these programs can be shaped in ways that directly and indirectly contribute to the development of democratic participation, which is valuable in itself and strengthens the foundation of change.
>
> (MacEwan 2003, pp. 6–7)[9]

Cash transfers, preferred by the mainstream, are generally less desirable for cost, efficiency, and equity reasons, except for emergency support to very poor groups and long-term assistance to the elderly, children, and the chronically sick and disabled, who have few alternative sources of income. For example, it is usually cheaper to provide public goods centrally, through public institutions, rather than privately via cash transfers (unless the domestic financial system is relatively sophisticated and bank cards are widely used) (Lavinas 2017). Moreover, cash transfers foster competition and the commodification of social life, which goes against the social solidarity pursued by DECS. In contrast, public goods and social wage programs ensure the provision of key goods and services to all, contribute to the decommodification of social exchange, and foster community relations.

Universal policies have a strongly progressive impact on gender, ethnic background, and other markers of "difference," which is valuable in itself, and which can help to reduce inequalities within the household and in society at large (Elson and Cagatay 2000; Perrons 2015). For example, minimum wage policies, equitable compensation for similar work, and old age pensions tend to benefit women more than men and Blacks more than Whites, because they tend to be overrepresented in the lowest-paid professions and work in informal labor markets (which generally lack protections, pensions, and health insurance), and because women generally live longer than men (Bhattacharya 2017; Chant and Pedwell 2008; Elson 1991). Building up equality is especially important in the face of climate change, which will require unprecedented levels of social cohesion to support the necessary policies of adaptation and mitigation, and to compensate the poor for the unavoidable privations to come.

In many countries, the administrative infrastructure to run universal programs is already in place, or it can be created relatively cheaply (MacEwan 2003; Saad-Filho 2007, 2011). These policies and programs can also be rolled out gradually (e.g., one product, service, diversification, or "green" initiative at a time); they can also be limited to selected regions, making them relatively simple to implement. Even where provision is universal, these programs can incorporate several advantages of targeted initiatives, a process that may be called "smart targeting": the programs are *universal* because they are available for all either to claim or to contribute to, and they are *targeted* because distinct social groups, genders, age cohorts, and so on will be affected differently by each project.[10] Similarly, conservation and diversification programs can focus on the gains to the poor; for example, employment creation programs can target deprived areas, regional development projects can create markets for local produce, and these initiatives can be linked to the expansion of infrastructure and the diversification of the sources of growth, for example, through public works (Chateau et al. 2018). At another level, governments can subsidize low-power electric motorcycles, which will be purchased mainly by the poor; restore vegetation on arid zones or mountainsides where the poor live; electrify railways used primarily by poor commuters; or drive volunteers to work in environmental projects benefiting the poor directly (Bhaduri et al. 2015). These initiatives can be articulated with larger public investment and housing programs, support to small-scale agriculture and small enterprises, and so on. In each case, the balance between the targeted and universal aspects of provision depends on policy decisions about impact, targets, access, and project costs.

Universal policies promoting gender, ethnic, and other equalities have been rejected by the mainstream because of their presumed lack of focus, high costs, inadequate targeting, and incentives to overconsumption (e.g., free health services could foster trivial complaints or unnecessary prescriptions; see, for example, OECD 2015). In turn, environmental programs may be wasteful (e.g., car scrappage schemes are notoriously vulnerable to distortions favoring the big automakers), while economic diversification initiatives can be captured by selfish or corrupt interests. Finally, universal programs deviate from the traditional mainstream focus on the reduction of wage differentials (Gebrewolde 2017). Although this focus is valuable, it may conceal a domestic reality of inequality and overwork especially for low income women, because of their caring responsibilities in addition to formal (or, often, informal) work outside the family home (Himmelweit 2017). This suggests that a broader approach may be better able to address discrimination and achieve the egalitarian goals of DECS (Perkins 2007; Seguino 2019; see also the special issue of *Feminist Economics* 26 from 2020).[11] For example, in addition to well-known discrimination, women also suffer disproportionately from the constraints of time and other basic resources, as well as from the lack of economic opportunities (Demaegdt 2017). A growing body of studies on the gender impact of energy access, mainly focusing on the Global South, reaches similar conclusions (Johnson et al. 2018; Kelkar and Nathan 2005; Oparaocha and Dutta 2011; Pachauri and Rao 2013; Ryan 2014)

Ignoring these differences in the target populations and the differential implications of economic policy would lead to inadequate or flawed understandings of poverty, inequality, and their structural implications, and could be conducive to the selection of ineffective or even perverse policies (Elson and Cagatay 2000; Gammage et al. 2020; Ross 2008). In contrast, when they are selected and monitored adequately, universal social policies and programs can have a strongly redistributive impact, promote equality, and support diversification and sustainability (UNDP 2013; UN Women 2015). They can also offer an invaluable contribution to the mitigation of climate change (Hujo 2012; Solati 2017; UNFCCC 2018b). It is similar with energy provision, which has been shown to promote gender equality, reduce poverty, and improve the position of women in society (Fathallah and Pyakurel 2020; Johnson et al. 2018; Lieu et al. 2020; Listo 2018; Pachauri and Rao 2013; Ryan 2014). In other words, in order to achieve a sustainable energy transition grounded in democratic principles, it is essential to identify the relevant feedback loops where DEPs can be most effective, and to intervene with focused, inclusive, and sensitive policies (that is, policies attuned to gender, ethnic, and other differentials). By the same token, it is known that the inclusion of gender and other types of diversity in decision-making tends to redistribute political power and encourage wider cultural, socioeconomic, and political changes (Johnson et al. 2018). In summary, and returning to gender inequalities as both significant in themselves and symptomatic of wider inequalities in society:

> [If] the "gender agenda" is ultimately about redressing that which is unfair and unjust and challenging unequal privilege, then … it is time to remove the mantle of acceptable euphemism that "gender" has provided and to talk much more directly about equality, rights

and power ... [W]hat is needed is a new narrative: one that can embrace ... concerns with women's rights, but steer clear of the essentialisms that have accompanied calls for women's empowerment; one that can go beyond the strictures of identity politics and provide the basis for broad-based alliances amongst those who identify with seeking an end to the injustice of unfair pay, unequal rights, discrimination and violence; and ultimately one that can convey the issues that matter in clear and unequivocal terms, rather than packaging them up in buzzwords.

(Cornwall 2007, pp. 76–77)

A sustainable path to economic development inspired by democratic values requires leaving no one behind; in turn, the complexity of poverty and the inequalities related to it imply the need to understand the feedback loops between them in order to engage in sensible policymaking. This approach applies across the spectrum of socially constructed inequalities that must be confronted by DECS, for example, those based on "race," sexual orientation, class, language and accent, "prestige," and other unacceptable grounds for discrimination. This is certainly an ambitious agenda, but it is essential to engage with it in order to overcome entrenched inequalities.

Notes

1 For an overview of tax rates in different countries, see https://ourworldinda ta.org/taxation.
2 "Cutting subsidies and increasing fuel taxes are politically difficult, but the recent spike and fall in oil and gas prices make the time opportune for doing so. Indeed, European countries used the 1974 oil crisis to introduce high fuel taxes ... Prices help explain why European emissions per capita (10 tons of CO_2e) are less than half those in the United States (23 tons). Global energy subsidies in developing countries were estimated at $310 billion in 2007, disproportionately benefiting higher-income populations ... But pricing is only one tool for advancing the energy-efficiency agenda, which suffers from market failures, high transaction costs, and financing constraints. Norms, regulatory reform, and financial incentives are also needed—and are cost-effective ... And because utilities are potentially effective delivery channels for making homes, commercial buildings, and industry more energy efficient, incentives have to be created for utilities to conserve energy. This can be done by decoupling a utility's profits from its gross sales, with profits instead increasing with energy conservation successes" (WDR 2010, pp. 14–15). For updated estimates of fossil fuel subsidies, see Coady et al. (2019).
3 The two-way relationship between financial sector structure and economic diversification is examined by Manganelli and Popov (2010, 2015).

4 See McKinley (2001). This line of causation is emphasized by the evolutionary and institutional literature on the "East Asian miracle"; see, for example, Amsden (1997).

5 "Since democracy and public involvement are usually regarded as fundamental for sustainability, existing social inequities based on gender and ethnicity must be addressed as part of any economic transition" (Perkins 2007, p. 234).

6 See Lim and Lim (2012) for a similar approach focusing on pro-poor outcomes. The choice of priorities in view of the need for rapid decarbonization is examined by Millward-Hopkins et al. (2020).

7 See also Alberola and Benigno (2017).

8 The examples of Ethiopia and Ghana are examined in IMF (2005); the case of Norway is reviewed by Akram (2004).

9 See also Danson et al. (2013); and Grosse et al. (2008). For example, Vandemoortele (2004, p. 12) notes: "While narrow targeting, user fees, and social investment funds can play a role, they can never be the mainstay of a country's anti-poverty strategy. In most contexts, they are likely to yield savings that are penny-wise but pound-foolish .... Despite the very modest amount of money they generate, user fees invariably lead to a reduction in the demand for services, particularly among the poor. Attempts to protect the poor—through exemptions or waivers—are seldom effective, although often expensive. The introduction of user fees also tends to aggravate gender discrimination ... [The abolition of] school fees in Malawi and Uganda and ... Kenya ... was followed by a surge in enrolment in all three countries—with girls being the prime beneficiaries. These positive experiences illustrate that even a small nominal fee can be a formidable obstacle for poor families."

10 For example, experiences in India and Brazil show that subsidized food stores and "popular restaurants" can be open to all while, at the same time, targeting the poor through their selection of products for sale (staple foods only) and the availability of the outlets (only in poor areas). The non-poor exclude themselves voluntarily: a middle-class Indian will not drive to a slum to purchase ordinary rice, and her Brazilian counterpart will never eat pork and beans in the company of her social inferiors, however cheap it may be.

11 "[T]he problem with 'gender equality' is more with what it disguises: the specificity of women's demands, whether for equal pay or reproductive rights ... 'women' is a descriptive term, one that can be filled with a diversity of meanings and mobilised for political ends by diverse actors, from neo-conservative promoters of 'family values' to radical feminists ... [Similarly,] anti-poverty programmes that are increasingly being spoken about as 'empowering' may end up reinforcing stereotypical roles for women as mothers' (Cornwall 2007, p. 75). Similarly, from an ecofeminist perspective, "[a] shared analysis, bringing together concerns for 'nature' and concerns for equity (including intraspecies, interspecies, and intergenerational balancing) is long overdue" (Perkins 2007, p. 228).

7 Financing the transition to an inclusive, diversified, and sustainable economy

Finance is likely to be one of the key challenges to a democratic strategy of economic development. This chapter examines possible sources of finance that can unlock an alternative approach to development that overcomes neoliberalism and addresses the impending climate disaster. The study focuses, in sequence, on domestic and external sources of finance, transfers, and the distribution of costs and gains across rich and poor both within and between countries.

Financing consumption and investment

Finance is likely to be a significant constraint to DECS, economic diversification and the mitigation of climate change (Ackerman et al. 2012; Gouvello et al. 2010; Khor 2011; UNFCCC 2007). Simply put, industrial, social, and environmental programs are expensive to run, and budgetary limitations should not be underestimated, especially in the DEs.

Conventional approaches to financing the mitigation of climate change assume that current output is divided into (a) consumption, which determines the welfare of the current generation; and (b) investment in new productive facilities, technology, and knowledge, which will expand the consumption possibilities of future generations. It follows that investments in DECS, economic diversification, and mitigation projects can be financed either through the compression of consumption (e.g., through taxes and fees) or through cuts in conventional investment funded out of current income, domestic loans, international borrowing, or external transfers. The conventional analysis of mitigation focuses on consumption. For example:

> According to the Intergovernmental Panel on Climate Change (IPCC) ... the cost of cutting global greenhouse gas emissions by

50 percent by 2050 could be in the range of 1–3 percent of GDP. That is the minimum cut most scientists believe is needed to have a reasonable chance of limiting global warming close to 2°C above preindustrial temperatures.

(WDR 2010, p. 259)

Taxes and fees will raise the price of carbon-intensive energy and, consequently, reduce real incomes and current consumption in order to fund investments benefiting future generations. The policy problem is how to achieve the maximum politically feasible compression of consumption in order to mobilize resources for "green" investments (De Bruin et al. 2009; Foley 2007; Nersisyan and Randall Wray 2019). It is expected that this would be resisted, for, in the words attributed to Groucho Marx, "why should I care about future generations—what have they ever done for me?"

This approach has been wholly insufficient to fund the investment required to address climate change, diversify poor economies, or distribute income. For example, given the target of 450 ppm of CO_2 in the atmosphere:

current levels of climate finance fall far short of foreseeable needs … [M]itigation costs in developing countries could reach \$140–\$175 billion a year by 2030 with associated financing needs of \$265–\$565 billion. Current flows of mitigation finance averaging some \$8 billion year to 2012 pale in comparison. And the estimated \$30–\$100 billion that could be needed annually [between 2010 and 2050] for adaptation in developing countries dwarfs the less than \$1 billion a year now available … These figures can be compared with current development assistance of roughly \$100 billion a year. Yet efforts to raise funding for mitigation and adaptation have been woefully inadequate, standing at less than 5 percent of projected needs.

(WDR 2010, pp. 22, 257)

There is no question that cuts in consumption will be necessary, for example through taxation, both to release resources and to reduce CO_2e emissions directly. This should be done in order to place the burden of emissions cuts squarely upon the rich and the AEs, since their consumption levels are much higher and more carbon-intensive per capita than those of the poor and the DEs (Beuret 2019; Colarossi 2015; Gore 2015; Turner 2020a). Whenever possible, these priorities should be funded primarily by domestic sources and by regulated international public funds, because private foreign savings and investment tend to be volatile and difficult to target, and they are often inimical to democratic goals. For example, foreign investors in poor countries often produce luxury goods and services rather than basic consumer goods and manufacturing inputs, and they frequently adopt environmentally damaging technologies.[1]

Raising the necessary resources domestically in poor countries will require a concerted effort, since the available savings tend to be insufficient to support ambitious development programs. Tax revenues will need to rise in most countries in order to help to fund these programs, which will demand a more progressive tax system, the taxation of unearned incomes and financial transactions, the taxation of part of the benefits of growth, and the redistribution of global taxes on "environmental sins" (see Chapter 6). It will also be necessary to set up or expand long-term public–private savings initiatives (such as development banks, as in Brazil and Chile), in order to fund infrastructure, housing, education, and training programs, pensions, and other costly distributive projects, and to fund projects focusing on climate mitigation and adaptation (Lim and Lim 2012; Marois 2021; UNCTAD 2019). In contrast, in very poor countries the savings potentially available domestically could be insufficient to permit the achievement of democratic development goals even under the best combination of policies. In this case, DECS will require additional resources through global tax and directed investments, aid, other unrequited transfers (such as workers' remittances) and debt forgiveness.[2]

This distributionally progressive approach to emissions, mitigation, and funding can be implemented through progressive "green" income taxes and surcharges; emergency taxes on capital gains and dividends; compulsory step-wise savings schemes; and steep taxes on carbon-intensive luxury goods (e.g., holidays, business-class travel, SUVs, and so on; see Davis and Caldeira 2010). They can be supplemented by Tobin-type taxes on financial transactions and international capital flows (that is, a tiny percentage tax on every transaction undertaken by banks or other financial institutions). These taxes would be difficult to evade and, as an added benefit, would "throw sand in the wheels" of financialization (Grahl and Lysandrou 2003; Wachtel 2000).

Additional resources to support DECS-led growth and economic diversification can be raised through domestic loans. It is generally accepted that investment funded by bank-created credit money in economies operating below capacity does not necessarily crowd out either consumption or other investments, while the loans can create jobs and promote the industrial policy and mitigation goals in DECS (see above). Loan finance can also transfer costs to future generations, which will benefit from those investments.[3] The added gain from borrowing to invest in diversification and mitigation is that they help to push the economy toward full employment, which creates labor scarcities that lift wages, benefiting the poor; in turn, rising interest rates would tend to dislocate low-return conventional investments (obviously the additional expenditures must taper off as the economy approaches full capacity). Since traditional investments would generally be based on already-existing comparative advantages (e.g., the oil sector) or on conventional (oil-intensive) consumption, their dislocation would support economic diversification and climate mitigation (for a similar argument, see Foley 2007).

In order to finance the domestic part of the required public investment programs, country governments must jettison the restrictive fiscal policy stance imposed by (P)WC policies. This will not necessarily be inflationary because, despite mainstream claims to the contrary, there is no clear or strong relationship between fiscal deficits and inflation (see, for example, Bordo and Levy 2020; Fischer et al. 2002; Terrones and Catão 2001; and Vieira 2000). As was mentioned above, public investment programs can be deficit-financed if the economy is operating below capacity, if the balance of payments constraint is not binding, and if the fiscal deficits can be financed in a sustainable manner (for example, if the additional public sector debt can be paid off by the tax revenues generated by future growth, or securely covered by foreign transfers). In these cases, public deficits should have no inflationary impact. However, if the government needs to monetize its deficit on a regular basis, perhaps because the financial markets are insufficiently developed, the expansion of demand must be regulated because of its potential implications for inflation, the exchange rate, and the balance of payments.

External sources of finance

Investment projects and their running costs, especially in key sectors to prevent lock-ins into carbon-intensive structures (transport, energy, and so on) can be funded by external loans and transfers (Hallegatte et al. 2016). For example, first, there should be global taxes on financial transactions, emissions, international transport (especially aviation and shipping), luxury consumption, and other "sins," and, in particular, a carbon tax with implementation based on CBDR:

> An equitable approach to limiting global emissions of greenhouse gases has to recognize that developing countries have legitimate

development needs, that their development may be jeopardized by climate change, and that they have contributed little, historically, to the problem.

(WDR 2010, p. 257)

Second, poor countries could benefit from the expansion of overseas development aid. This could be supplemented by the allocation of (to be introduced) oil extraction quotas to the poorest oil-export-dependent countries as part of an expanded global aid budget (in excess of the current global aid target of 0.7% of GDP). The reallocation of extraction permits to the poorer countries can be justified because they are small (Equatorial Guinea), their output is tiny relative to global demand (South Sudan), and some of these countries (Libya) do not currently have alternative sources of foreign exchange, implying that rapid cuts in oil exports would create severe hardship, requiring compensation by aid. In turn, larger countries with more diversified economies and higher per capita income (Norway, Russia, Saudi Arabia, United States) must accept diminished oil quotas in order to accommodate the right to development of the smaller and poorer ones (for a similar approach, see Lahn and Bradley 2016).

Third, poor countries could benefit from CBDR-compliant emissions permits, and/or from auctioning or taxing away assigned amount units (AAU), that is, the amount of carbon a country is permitted to emit under the Kyoto Protocol (WDR 2010). Another possible avenue of support for DEs involves the transfer of green technologies, including the establishment of global pools that would ideally managed by consortia or international organizations (Khor et al. 2017). They may be funded by direct transfers or aid, or through global taxes, and would accelerate the spread of appropriate technologies supporting the energy transition as well as retrofitting (EWG 2019).

Moving forward

Three objections are possible against the approach to finance outlined in this chapter. First, the traditional argument is that the required resources would reduce economic growth. It was shown above that this is incorrect: mitigation and diversification financed by borrowing can change the composition of investment but, in economies operating below capacity there is no reason to assume that it would reduce either total investment or aggregate consumption. Second, it could be argued that borrowing will ultimately (when the economy approaches full capacity) crowd out conventional investment by raising the interest rate. However, in the cases of mitigation of climate change and diversification away from oil, crowding out conventional investments is exactly what is needed. Third, it could be argued that there is insufficient political will in most countries to implement aggressive initiatives to reduce emissions and fund diversification. This is currently true; however, given the inertia of the Earth's climate, delays responding to the challenges of climate change and diversification will be castigated with steeply rising costs when action finally becomes unavoidable.

In summary, DECS require more expansionary fiscal policies funded by a much larger tax base. However, it is important to avoid exaggerating the relaxation of fiscal policy—but not because of groundless fears about crowding out or inflation. Loosening simultaneously fiscal, monetary, *and* exchange rate policies is potentially risky for three reasons. First, support for these "fully expansionary policies" draws upon a narrow reading of the experience of the United States and large Western European economies between the early twentieth century and the mid-1970s. These countries could either print the world currency (especially the United Kingdom before World War I and the United States after World War II), or they had easy access to foreign currency. This is hardly relevant to most DEs, whose balance of payments and environmental constraints are much tighter (see Chapter 3). Second, loose fiscal, monetary, *and* exchange rate policies could generate unsustainable booms that would be destabilizing both economically and politically. This is especially true for economies that are initially locked in stabilization traps—that is, starved of investment for long periods, and where high unemployment coexists with low spare capacity in key sectors (see Chapter 5). In these cases, a sudden policy reversal could trigger accelerating inflation and send the currency spiralling downward. Exactly the same outcomes could ensue in cases where the environmental constraint is binding, the country has been starved of investment, and the government launches a boom in "green growth." Third, the "fully" expansionary option is not always politically feasible. A sudden shift of the fiscal stance could become a lightning rod for the critics of the government's strategy, attracting the wrath of the IMF, World Bank, and the US Treasury Department and the local finance and mainstream media. This could undermine support for the government, trigger speculation with foreign currency or treasury bills, capital flight, inflation, and a balance of payments crisis even before the expansionary, distributive, and environmental impacts of the government's policies could be felt. In order to achieve the sought-after outcomes, fiscal policy should be calibrated in order to deliver what monetary and exchange rate policies cannot offer, especially in poor countries: targeted investment programs, incentives for private sector support to the democratic development strategy, and economic stabilization when this becomes necessary.

Notes

1 The suggestion that middle-income countries should rely primarily on domestic rather than on foreign savings is supported by the pioneering work of Feldstein and Horioka and Calvo, Leiderman, and Reinhart. For a heterodox interpretation of their findings, see Palma (1998).

2 "[T]he bulk of the extra investment in basic services and anti-poverty programmes will have to come from domestic resources, not from external sources. However, this does not diminish the marginal value of ODA. Indeed, foreign aid can play a critical role in overcoming obstacles in the transitory phase towards pro-poor policies since the latter are bound to meet stiff resistance from several quarters" (Vandemoortele 2004, p. 16).

3 "[There is a] widespread, but erroneous, belief that policies to reduce greenhouse gas emission will impose a cost on the current generation, which must be weighed against the benefits future generations will enjoy from mitigation ... [However, since] greenhouse gas emissions are an unpriced economic externality, this belief is incorrect ... The misperception that control of global warming is costly rests on the mistaken assumption that the investment allocation of the world economy without mitigation measures is efficient, but in the presence of an externality the world economy is not on its efficiency frontier" (Foley 2007, pp. 1–2).

Conclusion

This book has outlined the background to the climate crisis, and offered a menu of progressive policies to address economic diversification, redistribution, and environmental sustainability. It has shown that, across all channels of transmission, the impact of climate change will be felt primarily by the poor and the poorest countries by virtue of their greater vulnerability to any economic disruption.

Societies may be tempted to confront the outstanding tasks in sequence (presumably, first diversify, then grow, then redistribute), but this is unlikely to work in practice. On the one hand, the productive and distributional framework imposed by global neoliberalism binds the world economy to the production and consumption of fossil fuels: the economically dominant interests are locked into a logic of short-term financialized profit extraction that is incompatible with high-cost, long-term coordinated shifts in the composition of economic activity, the emergence of new drivers of accumulation, new sources of profit, and the redistribution of income. *Neoliberalism and financialization will drive the world economy into the abyss of environmental collapse and mass extinction.*

On the other hand, attempts to rebalance the global economy and redistribute income, wealth, and power within countries and between them while ignoring the environmental challenge will *also* drive the world over the edge. It is impossible to produce more and consume more everywhere, and equalize living standards upward ("global convergence") on the basis of existing technologies and those that can realistically be developed in the time available before climate change runs out of control: humans will not be in the world long enough to enjoy this imagined future. For reasons of efficiency, consistency, and legitimacy, our civilization must confront neoliberalism, financialization, and climate change *together* through a democratic economic strategy.

This approach is necessarily international: since the environment is global, it is essential to move away from nationalism in the formulation, implementation, and monitoring of economic policy. By the same token, countries no longer have the scope to choose policies that are "best for themselves," while externalizing their costs and damages. Inevitably, the Global South will have to shoulder a significant share of the burden of diversification and mitigation of climate change, and those countries must seek to self-fund and develop new appropriate technologies as much as possible. However, the principle of CBDR implies that the Global North must take primary responsibility for funding the worldwide transition, including the costs of diversification away from oil.

Although these heavy tasks have become unavoidable, the policies outlined in this book will not be implemented easily, given the lobby of the oil companies, the interests of large corporations, the timidity of most politicians, and the preferences of the privileged. They have profited from the current (neoliberal and financialized) structure of the world economy, and believe that wealth will protect them against the ravages of climate change. Yet, humans have never experienced a comparable challenge. While the Global North may escape wholesale devastation in the medium term, the dislocations in the South will be huge, with immediate consequences for countless lives and livelihoods. The necessary measures can find legitimacy and mass support *only* if they are coupled with improvements in distribution and the jettisoning of the income-concentrating logic of neoliberalism. Just like the promise of a more equal future gave force and legitimacy to the war effort against Nazi-fascism in the 1940s, today's world can find the strength to confront climate change only through a shared commitment to transcend neoliberalism.

Addressing climate change will be difficult not only for technical reasons, or even because of ideological prejudices. The main constraint is the structure of the global economy, which is based on the ruthless abuse of nature both for resources and as a sink for rejects from production and consumption. The deep roots of the climate crisis show that effective policies to combat it will be costly, complex, and resisted, since those policies must aim to transform the process of economic reproduction itself. Today's financialized societies are not merely "unprepared" to address the climate crisis: they have actively precipitated it while, at the same time, they have dismantled the institutional structures that could protect the current conditions supporting life on Earth. In other words, neoliberal capitalism has exposed humans and other living species to dangers and risks that it is unable to address or to contain.

The political process is central to the success of DECS on three levels. First, it will become possible to implement democratic policies only by removing the political chokehold of the traditional elites, who are committed to inequality and to unsustainable patterns of production, consumption, and economic growth, and by developing sustainable policies grounded in a universal citizenship. Second, political cooperation within and between countries is essential for the management of conflicts between sectional interests and the public good. Third, the political weakness of the poor and the poor countries can be overcome only through their mobilization around important causes, and nothing is more important than collective survival. In this sense, the DEs and the poor can lead the transformation of the world economy beyond neoliberalism, and steer the globe away from environmental disaster.

The political mobilization of poor people should be welcomed, because it will directly express the interests of the majority, help to offset the political biases toward the rich built under neoliberalism, and give leverage to governments committed to DECS. While the potential costs and inefficiencies of public policy are often used to justify the preservation of an unsustainable status quo, the opposite must now become true: the majority of the population in most countries must mobilize in order to make the costs of avoiding redistribution, diversification, mitigation, and sustainability prohibitively high.[1] This is not a novelty. The political mobilization of the poor in the United Kingdom in the late nineteenth century helped to reduce inequalities in that country, and mobilizations in Western Europe and East Asia after World War II brought significant gains to the majority.

Today, the *only* legitimate way to select the appropriate targets and government policy tools is by involving civil society in the choice, implementation, and assessment of macroeconomic policy. This is especially important because the challenges and the desired outcomes are complex, diverse, and controversial, and because macroeconomic policy is limited by overlapping constraints. Several potential tools are available to help achieve given goals, and there is a non-linear relationship between economic circumstances, policies, and outcomes. Debates about macroeconomic policy goals and tools should be welcomed, because they will help to break the monopoly of the moneyed interests, professional politicians, paid advisors, lobbyists, and established academics in the selection, implementation, and evaluation of economic policy. Paraphrasing Milton Friedman, and many others before him, *economic policy is too important to be left to the policymakers.*

The expansion of economic and political democracy requires the extension of the political sphere and the reconstruction of public policymaking and managerial capacities in the wake of the neoliberal "reforms" associated with neoliberalism and the (P)WC. This will require, among other things, dismantling the (partly or wholly privatized) administrative and policy structures that currently rival the state institutions, and reducing the interference of foreign governments, NGOs, and international organizations in the selection, management, and appraisal of investment programs, even if they are aid-funded. The expansion of the realm of politics does not imply that the state should aim to "seize" assets or "take over" the economy: DECS are distinctive not because the state manages individual firms, but because of the way in which the state coordinates economic activity for democratic, distributive, and sustainable ends. State ownership of specific assets is a secondary issue; what matters are the objectives of government policy, and how state institutions interact with one another and with private concerns. This is an argument for *specificity* in DECS. The diversity of country experiences over time suggests that the state and its economic policies cannot be selected or analyzed in the abstract. Similarly, there can be no expectation that policies can be replicated from one country to another with the same effects. Historical instances of success and failure must be assessed in context, recognizing that their outcomes are specific to country and time.

Despite the urgency of these tasks, most countries, companies, and households have tended to avoid decisive action, which only increases the severity of the problem and the sharpness of the inevitable "hand-brake turn" coming in the near future. There is still time, but, it seems, only just. The time for action is now.

Note

1 For a similar argument, see McKinley (2009).

References

Abbas, S. (2014), "Trade Liberalization and Its Economic Impact on Developing and Least Developed Countries," *Journal of International Trade Law and Policy* 13 (3), pp. 215–221.

Acemoglu, D. and Robinson, J.A. (2006), *Economic Origins of Dictatorship and Democracy*. Cambridge: Cambridge University Press.

Ackerman, F., Kozul-Wright, R., and Vos, R. (2012), *Climate Protection and Development*. New York: Bloomsbury Academic.

Adam, C. (2013), "Dutch Disease and Foreign Aid," in S.N. Durlauf and L.E. Blume (eds.), *The New Palgrave Dictionary of Economics*, pp. 3116–3124. London: Palgrave Macmillan.

Agosín, M.R. and Tussie, D. (eds.) (1993), *Trade and Growth: New Dilemmas in Trade Policy*. London: Macmillan.

Ahmadov, A. (2012), *Political Determinants of Economic Diversification in Natural Resource Rich Developing Countries*, Princeton University, May 4, https://www.academia.edu/12449300/Political_Determinants_of_Economic_ Diversification_in_Natural_Resource-Rich_Developing_Countries.

Ahrend, R. (2008), *Strategies for Economic Diversification in the Resource-Rich Countries?*Organisation for Economic Cooperation and Development, April 4, https://www.un.org/en/development/desa/policy/publications/general_assembly/ eitconference/4apram_ahrend.pdf.

Ait-Laoussine, N. and Gault, J. (2017), "Nationalization, Privatization and Diversification," *Journal of World Energy Law and Business*, 10 (1), pp. 43–54.

Akram, Q.F. (2004), *Oil Wealth and Real Exchange Rates: The FEER for Norway*, Money Macro and Finance (MMF) Research Group Conference 2004 #33. https://ideas.repec.org/p/mmf/mmfc04/33.html.

Alami, I. (2020), *Post-Crisis Capital Controls in Developing Countries: Regaining Policy Space?*, PPESydney. March 15. http://ppesydney.net/post-crisis-capital-controls-in-developing-economies-regaining-policy-space/.

Alberola, E. and Benigno, G. (2017), "Revisiting the Commodity Curse: A Financial Perspective," *Journal of International Economics* 108 (S1), pp. 87–106.

Alexeev, M. and Conrad, R. (2009), "The Elusive Curse of Oil," *Review of Economics and Statistics* 91 (3), pp. 586–598.

Alfano, M.R. and Baraldi, A.L. (2016), "Democracy, Political Competition and Economic Growth," *Journal of International Development* 28 (8), pp. 1199–1219.

Alsharif, N. (2017), "Three Essays on Growth and Economic Diversification in Resource Rich Countries," PhD Dissertation, University of Sussex.

Alsharif, N., Bhattacharyya, S., and Intartaglia, M. (2017), "Economic Diversification in Resource Rich Countries: History, State of Knowledge and Research Agenda," *Resources Policy* 52, pp. 154–164.

Alvaredo, F., Chancel, L., Piketty, T., Saez, E., and Zucman, G. (2018), *World Inequality Report*, World Inequality Lab, https://wir2018.wid.world/files/download/wir2018-full-report-english.pdf.

Amsden, A. (1997), "Bringing Production Back In," *World Development* 25 (4), pp. 469–480.

Amsden, A. (2001), *The Rise of the Rest: Challenges to the West from Late Industrializing Economies.* Oxford: Oxford University Press.

Anderson, E., D'Orey, M.A.J., Duvendack, M., and Esposito, L. (2016), "Does Government Spending Affect Income Inequality? A Meta-Regression Analysis," *Journal of Economic Surveys* 31 (4), pp. 961–987.

Anderson, K., Broderick, J.F., and Stoddard, I. (2020), "A Factor of Two: How the Mitigation Plans of 'Climate Progressive' Nations Fall Far Short of Paris-Compliant Pathways," *Climate Policy* 20 (10), pp. 1290–1304.

Ansari, D. and Holz, F. (2020), "Between Stranded Assets and Green Transformation," *World Development* 130, doi:10.1016/j.worlddev.2020.104947.

Arrighi, G. (1994), *The Long Twentieth Century.* London: Verso.

Arsel, M., Hogenboom, B., and Pellegrini, L. (2016), "The Extractive Imperative in Latin America," *Extractive Industries and Society* 3 (4), pp. 880–887.

Ashman, S. and Fine, B. (2013), "Neo-Liberalism, Varieties of Capitalism, and the Shifting Contours of South Africa's Financial System," *Transformation* 81–82, pp. 144–178.

Auty, R.M. (2001), *Economic Development and Industrial Policy: Korea, Brazil, Mexico, India and China.* London: Mansell.

Baer, H.A. (2012), *Global Capitalism and Climate Change: The Need for an Alternative World System.* Lanham, MD: AltaMira Press.

Balakrishnan, R., Elson, D., and Patel, R. (2010), *Rethinking Macro Economic Strategies from a Human Rights Perspective*, Rutgers University, https://www.cwgl.rutgers.edu/docman/economic-and-social-rights-publications/20-whymeswithhumanrights2-pdf/file.

Barrowclough, D.V. and Kozul-Wright, R. (2018a), "Integrated Industrial Policy," in M.A. Yülek (ed.), *Industrial Policy and Sustainable Growth*, pp. 51–68. Singapore: Springer.

Barrowclough, D.V. and Kozul-Wright, R. (2018b), "Institutional Geometry of Industrial Policy in Sustainable Development," in M.A. Yülek (ed.), *Industrial Policy and Sustainable Growth*, pp. 85–108. Singapore: Springer.

Bateman, M. (2010), *Why Doesn't Microfinance Work? The Destructive Rise of Local Neoliberalism*. London: Zed Press.

Bateman, M. (2014), "South Africa's Post-Apartheid Microcredit Driven Calamity," *Law, Democracy and Development* 18, pp. 92–135.

Bateman, M., Blankenburg, S., and Kozul-Wright, R. (eds.) (2018), *The Rise and Fall of Global Microcredit: Development, Debt and Disillusion*. London: Routledge.

Baunsgaard, T., Villafuerte, M., Poplawski-Ribeiro, M., and Richmond, C. (2012), *Fiscal Frameworks for Resource Rich Developing Countries*, International Monetary Fund, May 16, https://www.imf.org/external/pubs/ft/sdn/2012/sdn1204.pdf.

Beaverstock, J., Hall, S., and Wainwright, T. (2013), "Servicing the Super-Rich: New Financial Elites and the Rise of the Private Wealth Management Retail Ecology," *Regional Studies* 47 (6), pp. 834–849.

Bendell, J. (2018), *Deep Adaptation: A Map for Navigating Climate Tragedy*, http://insight.cumbria.ac.uk/id/eprint/4166/.

Berg, A., Buffie, E.F., Pattillo, C., … and Zanna, L.-F. (2015), *Some Misconceptions about Public Investment Efficiency and Growth*, Working Paper #15/272, International Monetary Fund, December. https://www.imf.org/external/pubs/ft/wp/2015/wp15272.pdf.

Besley, T. and Cord, L.J. (eds.) (2007), *Delivering on the Promise of Pro-Poor Growth: Insights and Lessons from Country Experiences*, Washington, DC: World Bank.

Beuret, N. (2019), *Emissions Inequality: There Is a Gulf between Global Rich and Poor*, The Conversation, March 28. https://theconversation.com/emissions-inequality-there-is-a-gulf-between-global-rich-and-poor-113804.

Bhaduri, A., Banerjee, K., and Moughari, Z.K. (2015), "Fight against Unemployment: Rethinking Public Works Programs," *Real-World Economics Review* 72, pp. 174–185.

Bhattacharya, T. (ed.) (2017), *Social Reproduction Theory*. London: Pluto Press.

Bloch, D., Fournier, J.M., Gonzales, D., and Pina, A. (2016), *Trends in Public Finances: Insights from a New Detailed Dataset*, Working Paper #1345, Organisation for Economic Co-Operation and Development, November. https://ideas.repec.org/p/oec/ecoaaa/1345-en.html.

Bordo, M.D. and Levy, M.D. (2020), *Do Enlarged Fiscal Deficits Cause Inflation: The Historical Record*, Working Paper #28195, National Bureau of Economic Research, December. https://www.hoover.org/sites/default/files/research/docs/20124-bordo-levy.pdf.

Bos, K. and Gupta, J. (2019), "Stranded Assets and Stranded Resources: Implications for Climate Change Mitigation and Global Sustainable Development," *Energy Research and Social Science* 56, doi:10.1016/j.erss.2019.05.025.

Boyce, J. (2004), *Green and Brown? Globalization and the Environment*, Working Paper #2004-01, Department of Economics, University of Massachusetts, https://www.umass.edu/economics/publications/2004-01.pdf.

Branco, M.C. (2012), "Economics against Democracy," *Review of Radical Political Economics* 44 (1), pp. 23–39.

Brenton, P., Gillson, I., and Sauvé, P. (2019), "Economic Diversification: Lessons from Practice," in *Aid for Trade at a Glance 2019: Economic Diversification and Empowerment*, pp. 135–160. Paris: OECD.

Bruszt, L. (2006), "Making Capitalism Compatible with Democracy: Tentative Reflections from the 'East'," in C. Crouch and W. Streeck (eds.), *The Diversity of Democracy*, pp. 149–172. Cheltenham, UK: Edward Elgar.

Bumann, S. and Lensink, R. (2013), *Financial Liberalization and Income Inequality: Channels and Cross-Country Evidence*, https://assets.publishing.service.gov.uk/media/57a08a3de5274a31e00004d2/61070_BaumannLensink.pdf.

Bush, G. (2019), "Financial Development and the Effects of Capital Controls," *Open Economics Review* 30, pp. 559–592.

Callen, T., Cherif, R., Hasanov, F. ..., and Khandelwal, P. (2014), *Economic Diversification in the GCC: Past, Present, and Future*, International Monetary Fund, December, https://www.imf.org/external/pubs/ft/sdn/2014/sdn1412.pdf.

Cammack, P. (2004), "What the World Bank Means by Poverty Reduction, and Why It Matters," *New Political Economy* 9 (2), pp. 189–211.

Campos-Vazquez, R., Chavez, E., and Esquivel, G. (2017), "Growth Is (Really) Good for the (Really) Rich," *The World Economy* 40 (12), pp. 2639–2675.

Carmignani, F. and Mandeville, T. (2014), "Never Been Industrialized: A Tale of African Structural Change," *Structural Change and Economic Dynamics* 31, pp. 124–137.

Caselli, F., Koren, M., Lisicky, M., and Tenreyro, S. (2015), *Diversification through Trade*, Working Paper #21498, National Bureau of Economic Research, August, https://www.nber.org/papers/w21498.

CGD (2008), *The Growth Report: Strategies for Sustained Growth and Inclusive Development*. Washington, DC: World Bank.

Chang, H.-J. (1994), *The Political Economy of Industrial Policy*. London: Macmillan.

Chang, H.-J. and Grabel, I. (2004), *Reclaiming Development: An Alternative Economic Policy Manual*. London: Zed Books.

Chant, S. and Pedwell, C. (2008), *Women, Gender and the Informal Economy*, International Labour Organization. http://www.cpahq.org/cpahq/cpadocs/wcms091228.pdf.

Chateau, J., Bibas, R., and Lanzi, E. (2018), *Impacts of Green Growth Policies on Labour Markets and Wage Income Distribution*, Working Paper #137, Organisation for Economic Co-Operation and Development, November. https://www.oecd-ilibrary.org/environment/impacts-of-green-growth-policies-on-labour-markets-and-wage-income-distribution_ea3696f4-en.

Chesnais, F. (2016), *Finance Capital Today*. Leiden: Brill.

Christophers, B. and Fine, B. (2019), "The Value of Financialization and the Financialization of Value," in P. Mader, D. Mertens and N. van der Zwan (eds.), *International Handbook of Financialization*, pp. 19–30. London: Routledge.

Coady, D., Parry, I., Le, N.-P., and Shang, B. (2019), *Global Fossil Fuel Subsidies Remain Large: An Update Based on Country-Level Estimates*, International Monetary Fund, May 2. https://www.imf.org/en/Publications/WP/Issues/2019/05/02/Global-Fossil-Fuel-Subsidies-Remain-Large-An-Update-Based-on-Country-Level-Estimates-46509.

Colarossi, J. (2015), *The World's Richest People Emit the Most Carbon*, Our World, December. https://ourworld.unu.edu/en/the-worlds-richest-people-also-emit-the-most-carbon.

Collier, P. and Hoeffler, A. (2005), "Resource Rents, Governance, and Conflict," *Journal of Conflict Resolution* 49 (4), pp. 625–633.

Consoli, C.P. and Wildgust, N. (2017), "Current Status of Global Storage Resources," *Energy Procedia* 114, pp. 4623–4628.

Corbera, E., Costedoat, S., Ezzine-de-Blas, D., and Van Hecken, G. (2019), "Troubled Encounters: Payments for Ecosystem Services in Chiapas, Mexico," *Development and Change* 51 (1), pp. 167–195.

Corden, M. and Neary, J.P. (1982), "Booming Sector and Deindustrialization in a Small Open Economy," *Economic Journal* 92 (368), pp. 825–848.

Cornia, G. (ed.) (2006), *Pro-Poor Macroeconomics: Potential and Limitations.* Houndmills, UK: Palgrave.

Cornia, G. and Martorano, B. (2012), *Development Policies and Income Inequality in Selected Developing Regions, 1980–2010*, United Nations Conference on Trade and Development, December, https://unctad.org/en/PublicationsLibrary/osgdp20124_en.pdf.

Cornwall, A. (2007), "Revisiting the Gender Agenda," *IDS Bulletin* 38 (2), pp. 69–78.

Cowell, F.A. and Van Kerm, P. (2015), "Wealth Inequality: A Survey," *Journal of Economic Surveys* 29 (4), pp. 671–710.

Cozzi, G. and Nissanke, M. (2009), *Capital Controls and the Current Financial Crisis: Revisiting the Malaysian Experience*, Centre for Development Policy and Research, Development Viewpoint 35, https://www.soas.ac.uk/cdpr/publications/dv/file53082.pdf.

Craig, D. and Porter, D. (2003), "Poverty Reduction Strategy Papers: A New Convergence," *World Development* 31 (1), pp. 53–69.

Craig, D. and Porter, D. (2006), *Development beyond Neoliberalism?* Abingdon, UK: Routledge.

Dagdeviren, H., van der Hoeven, R., and Weeks, J. (2002), "Poverty Reduction with Growth and Redistribution," *Development and Change* 33 (3), pp. 383–413.

Danson, M., McAlpine, R., Spicker, P., and Sullivan, W. (2013), *The Case for Universalism: Assessing the Evidence*, Centre for Labour and Social Studies, April. http://classonline.org.uk/pubs/item/the-case-for-universalism.

Davis, G.A. (1995), "Learning to Love the Dutch Disease: Evidence from the Mineral Economies," *World Development* 23 (10), pp. 1765–1779.

Davis, S.J. and Caldeira, K. (2010), "Consumption-Based Accounting of CO2 Emissions," *Proceedings of the National Academy of Sciences of the United States of America* 107 (12), pp. 5687–5692.

De Bruin, K., Dellink, R., and Agrawala, S. (2009), *Economic Aspects of Adaptation to Climate Change: Integrated Assessment Modelling of Adaptation Costs and Benefits*, Working Paper #6, Organisation for Economic Co-Operation and Development, March 24. https://www.oecd-ilibrary.org/environment/economic-aspects-of-adaptation-to-climate-change_225282538105.

Demaegdt, F. (2017), *From Victims to Actors: Women's Inclusion in the Energy Transition*, Geneva: Graduate Institute of International and Development Studies.

Demaria, F., Schneider, F., Sekulova, F., and Martinez-Alier, J. (2013), "What Is Degrowth?" *Environmental Values* 22, pp. 191–215.

Dercon, S. (2014), *Is Green Growth Good for the Poor?* Oxford University, October. http://www.espa.ac.uk/files/espa/Greengrowth.pdf.

Detchon, R. and Van Leeuwen, R. (2014), "Bring Sustainable Energy to the Developing World," *Nature* 508, pp. 309–311.

Dhir, S. and Dhir, S. (2015), "Diversification: Literature Review and Issues," *Strategic Change* 24 (6), pp. 569–588.

Ding, N. and Field, B.C. (2005), "Natural Resource Abundance and Economic Growth," *Land Economics* 81 (4), pp. 496–502.

Diop, N., Marotta, D., and de Melo, J. (2012), *Natural Resource Abundance, Growth & Diversification in MENA*, World Bank, September 8, http://documents.worldbank.org/curated/en/362691468278937113/Natural-resource-abundance-growth-and-diversification-in-the-Middle-East-and-North-Africa-the-effects-of-natural-resources-and-the-role-of-policies.

Dorn, F. and Schinke, C. (2018), "Top Income Shares in OECD Countries: The Role of Government Ideology and Globalisation," *The World Economy* 41 (9), pp. 2491–2527.

Dreher, A. (2006), "IMF and Economic Growth: The Effects of Programs, Loans, and Compliance with Conditionality," *World Development* 34 (5), pp. 769–788.

ECLAC (2017), "Economic Diversification," *Focus* 2, pp. 3–4, https://repositorio.cepal.org/bitstream/handle/11362/42399/FOCUSIssue2Apr-Jun2017.pdf.

Eichengreen, B. and Rose, A. (2014), "Capital Controls in the 21st Century," *Journal of International Money and Finance* 48, pp. 1–16.

Elson, D. (1991), *Male Bias in the Development Process*. Manchester: Manchester University Press.

Elson, D. and Cagatay, N. (2000), "The Social Content of Macroeconomic Policies," *World Development* 28 (7), pp. 1347–1364.

Epstein, G. (ed.) (2005), *Capital Flight and Capital Controls in Developing Countries*. Cheltenham, UK: Edward Elgar.

Erixon, L. (2018), "Progressive Supply-Side Economics: An Explanation and Update of the Rehn-Meidner Model," *Cambridge Journal of Economics* 42 (3), pp. 653–697.

Esanov, A. (2012), *Diversification in Resource Dependent Countries: Its Dynamics and Policy Issues*, Natural Resource Governance Institute, June 6, https://resourcegovernance.org/analysis-tools/publications/diversification-resource-dependent-countries.

Escaith, H. and Tamenu, B. (2014), "Surfing on the Tide? Least-Developed Countries Trade during the Great Global Transition," *Theoretical and Practical Research in Economic Field* 1 (9), pp. 32–48.

ETC (2018), *Mission Possible: Reaching Net-Zero Carbon Emissions from Harder-to-Abate Sectors by Mid-Century*, https://www.energy-transitions.org/publications/mission-possible/.

EWG (2019), *Global Energy System Based on 100% Renewable Energy*, http://energywatchgroup.org/new-study-global-energy-system-based-100-renewable-energy.

Fardmanesh, M. (1991), "Dutch Disease Economics and the Oil Syndrome: An Empirical Study," *World Development* 19 (6), pp. 711–717.

Fathallah, J. and Pyakurel, P. (2020), "Addressing Gender in Energy Studies," *Energy Research & Social Science* 65, doi:10.1016/j.erss.2020.101461.

Ficklin, L., Stringer, L.C., Dougill, A.J., and Sallu, S.M. (2018), "Climate Compatible Development Reconsidered: Calling for a Critical Perspective," *Climate and Development* 10 (3), pp. 193–196.

Fine, B. (2013–2014), "Financialisation from a Marxist Perspective," *International Journal of Political Economy* 42 (4), pp. 47–66.

Fine, B., Lapavitsas, C., and Pincus, J. (eds.) (2001), *Development Policy in the Twenty-First Century: Beyond the Post-Washington Consensus*. London: Routledge.

Fine, B. and Saad-Filho, A. (2014), "Politics of Neoliberal Development: Washington Consensus and Post-Washington Consensus," in H. Weber (ed.), *The Politics of Development: A Survey*, pp. 154–166. London: Routledge.

Fine, B. and Saad-Filho, A. (2017), "Thirteen Things You Need to Know about Neoliberalism," *Critical Sociology* 43 (4–5), pp. 685–706.

Fine, B. and Van Waeyenberge, E. (2006), "Correcting Stiglitz: From Information to Power in the World of Development," *Socialist Register* 42, pp. 146–168. Fischer, S., Sahay R., and Végh, C. (2002), *Modern Hyper- and High Inflations*, Working Paper #02/107, International Monetary Fund, November. https://www.imf.org/external/pubs/ft/wp/2002/wp02197.pdf.

Foley, D.K. (2007), *The Economic Fundamentals of Global Warming*, Working Paper #2007-12-044, Santa Fe Institute, October. https://www.santafe.edu/research/results/working-papers/the-economic-fundamentals-of-global-warming.

Fontana, G. and Sawyer, M. (2016), "Towards Post-Keynesian Ecological Macroeconomics," *Ecological Economics* 121, pp. 186–195.

Fossil Fuel Finance Report (2020), *Banking on Climate Change*, https://www.ran.org/bankingonclimatechange2020/.

Fossil Fuel Report Card (2016), *Shorting the Climate*, http://priceofoil.org/2016/06/15/shorting-the-climate/.

Foster, J.B. and Clark, B. (2020), *The Robbery of Nature: Capitalism and the Ecological Rift*. New York: Monthly Review Press.

Fournier, J.M. (2016), *The Positive Effect of Public Investment on Potential Growth*, Working Paper #1347, Organisation for Economic Co-Operation and Development, November. https://www.oecd-ilibrary.org/economics/the-positive-effect-of-public-investment-on-potential-growth_15e400d4-en?crawler=true.

Fournier, J.M. and Johansson, A. (2016), *The Effect of the Size and the Mix of Public Spending on Growth and Inequality*, Working Paper #1344, Organisation for Economic Co-Operation and Development, December. https://www.oecd-ilibrary.org/economics/the-effect-of-the-size-and-the-mix-of-public-spending-on-growth-and-inequality_f99f6b36-en.

Freire, C. (2017), *Economic Diversification: Explaining the Pattern of Diversification in the Global Economy and Its Implications for Fostering Diversification in Poorer Countries*, United Nations, Department of Economics and Social Affairs, August, https://ideas.repec.org/p/une/wpaper/150.html.

Furman, J. and Podesta, J. (2014), *New Report: The Cost of Delaying Action to Stem Climate Change*, Obama White House Archives, July 29, https://obamawhitehouse.archives.gov/blog/2014/07/29/new-report-cost-delaying-action-stem-climate-change.

Galbraith, J.K. (2011), "Inequality and Economic and Political Change: A Comparative Perspective," *Cambridge Journal of Regions, Economy and Society*, 4 (1), pp. 13–27.

Gammage, S., Joshi, S., and Rodgers, Y. (2020), "The Intersections of Women's Economic and Reproductive Empowerment," *Feminist Economics* 26 (1), pp. 1–22.

Gaulin, N. and Le Billon, P. (2020), "Climate Change and Fossil Fuel Production Cuts: Assessing Global Supply-Side Constraints and Policy Implications," *Climate Policy* 20 (8), pp. 888–901.

Gebrewolde, T.M. (2017), *The Global Gender Gap in Labor Income*, Division of Economics, School of Business, University of Leicester, July. https://econpapers.repec.org/RePEc:lec:leecon:17/14.

Gelb, A. (2010), *Economic Diversification in Resource Rich Countries*, International Monetary Fund, https://www.imf.org/external/np/seminars/eng/2010/afrfin/pdf/Gelb2.pdf.

Gençsü, I., Whitley, S., Trilling, M. …, and Worrall, L. (2020), "Phasing Out Public Financial Flows to Fossil Fuel Production in Europe," *Climate Policy* 20 (8), pp. 1010–1023.

Gerber, J.-D., and Gerber, J.-F. (2017), "Decommodification as a Foundation for Ecological Economics," *Ecological Economics* 131, pp. 551–556.

Gereffi, G. and Wyman, D.L. (eds.) (1990), *Manufacturing Miracles: Paths of Industrialization in Latin America and East Asia*. Princeton, NJ: Princeton University Press.

Germain, M. (2017), "Optimal versus Sustainable Degrowth Policies," *Ecological Economics* 136, pp. 266–281.

Gerschenkron, A. (1962), *Economic Backwardness in Historical Perspective*. Cambridge, MA: Harvard University Press.

Ghosh, J. (2012), "Redefining Development and Quality of Life', *Economic and Political Weekly* 47 (7), pp. 37–43.

Ghosh, J. (2015), "Beyond the Millennium Development Goals: A Southern Perspective on a Global New Deal," *Journal of International Development* 27, pp. 320–329.

Goda, T. and P. Lysandrou (2013), "The Contribution of Wealth Concentration to the Subprime Crisis: A Quantitative Estimation," *Cambridge Journal of Economics* 38 (2), pp. 301–327.

Golub, S. and Prasad, V. (2016), *Promoting Economic Diversification and International Competitiveness in Angola*, Swarthmore College, April, https://www.swarthmore.edu/sites/default/files/assets/documents/user_profiles/sgolub1/AngolaStudyTrade2016.rev2_.pdf.

Gore, T. (2015), *Extreme Carbon Inequality*, Oxfam International, September 21. https://www.oxfam.org/en/research/extreme-carbon-inequality.

Gouvello, C., Zelenko, I., and Ambrosi, P. (2010), *A Financing Facility for Low-Carbon Development*, Working Paper #203, World Bank. https://elibrary.worldbank.org/doi/abs/10.1596/978-0-8213-8521-0.

Gowan, P. (1999), *The Global Gamble: America's Faustian Bid for World Dominance*. Verso: London.

Grabel, E. (2004), *Trip Wires and Speed Bumps: Managing Financial Risks and Reducing the Potential for Financial Crises in Developing Economies*, G-24 Discussion Paper #33, United Nations Conference on Trade and Development. https://ideas.repec.org/p/unc/g24pap/33.html.

Grahl, J. and Lysandrou, P. (2003), "Sand in the Wheels or Spanner in the Works? The Tobin Tax and Global Finance," *Cambridge Journal of Economics* 27 (4), pp. 597–621.

Granados, J.A.T. (2018), "Inexorable March toward Utter Climate Disaster?" *Capitalism Nature Socialism* 29 (4), pp. 21–30.

Grant, A. (2020), *Handbrake Turn: The Cost of Failing to Anticipate an Inevitable Policy Response to Climate Change*, https://carbontracker.org/reports/handbrake-turn/.

Greenleaf, M. (2019), "Rubber and Carbon: Opportunity Costs, Incentives and Ecosystem Services in Acre, Brazil," *Development and Change* 51 (1), pp. 51–72.

Grosse, M., Harttgen, K., and Klasen, S. (2008), "Measuring Pro-Poor Growth in Non-Income Dimensions," *World Development* 36 (6), pp. 1021–1047.

Gunter, B.G., Cohen, M.J., and Lofgren, H. (2005), "Analysing Macro-Poverty Linkages: An Overview," *Development Policy Review* 23 (3), pp. 243–265.

Haglund, D. (2011), *Blessing or Curse? The Rise of Mineral Dependence among Low-and Middle-Income Countries*, Oxford Policy Management, December, https://eiti.org/document/opm-study-blessing-curse-rise-of-mineral-dependence-among-low-middleincome-countries.

Hahnel, R. (2012), "Left Clouds over Climate Change Policy," *Review of Radical Political Economics* 44 (2), pp. 141–159.

Hailu, D and Kipgen, C. (2017), "The Extractives Dependence Index (EDI)," *Resources Policy* 51, pp. 251–264.

Hall, A. (2004), *Extractive Reserves: Building Natural Assets in the Brazilian Amazon*, Political Economy Research Institute, University of Massachusetts, January 1, https://www.peri.umass.edu/publication/item/94-extractive-reserves-building-natural-assets-in-the-brazilian-amazon.

Hallegatte, S., Bangalore, M., Bonzanigo, L., . . . and Vogt-Schilb, A. (2016), *Shock Waves: Managing the Impacts of Climate Change on Poverty.* Washington, DC: World Bank.

Hamdaoui, M. and Maktouf, S. (2019), "Overall Effects of Financial Liberalization: Financial Crisis versus Economic Growth," *International Review of Applied Economics* 33 (4), pp. 568–595.

Hansen, J., Sato, M., Kharecha, P. . . . and Zachos, J. (2008), "Target Atmospheric CO2: Where Should Humanity Aim?" in B. McKibben (ed.), *The Global Warming Reader: A Century of Writing about Climate Change*, pp. 81–88. London: Penguin.

Harrison, A., McLaren, J., and McMillan, M. (2011), "Recent Perspectives on Trade and Inequality," *Annual Review of Economics* 3, pp. 261–289.

Harriss-White, B. (2005), *Poverty and Capitalism*, Working Paper #134, Queen Elizabeth House, Oxford, http://workingpapers.qeh.ox.ac.uk/RePEc/qeh/qehwps/qehwps134.pdf.

Hausmann, R. and Hidalgo, C.A. (2011), "The Network Structure of Economic Output," *Journal of Economic Growth* 16 (4), pp. 309–342.

Hausmann, R. and Klinger, B. (2007), *The Structure of the Product Space and the Evolution of Comparative Advantage*, Working Paper 146, Center for International Development, Harvard University, https://www.hks.harvard.edu/centers/cid/publications/faculty-working-papers/structure-product-space-and-evolution-comparative-advantage.

HDR (2002), *Human Development Report: Deepening Democracy in a Fragmented World*, http://hdr.undp.org/sites/default/files/reports/263/hdr_2002_en_complete.pdf.

He, J. (2019), "Situated Payments for Ecosystem Services: Local Agencies in the Implementation of the Sloping Land Conversion Programme in Southwest China," *Development and Change* 51 (1), pp. 73–93.

Heltberg, R. (2004), "The Growth Elasticity of Poverty," in A. Shorrocks and R. van der Hoeven (eds.), *Growth, Inequality, and Poverty: Prospects for Pro-Poor Economic Development*, pp. 81–91. Oxford: Oxford University Press.

Hendrix, C.S. (2017), *Kicking a Crude Habit: Diversifying Away from Oil and Gas in the 21st Century*, Working Paper #17-2, Petersen Institute for international Economics, https://www.ssrn.com/abstract=2912333.

Hesse, H. (2008), *Export Diversification and Economic Growth*, Working Paper #21, World Bank, https://openknowledge.worldbank.org/handle/10986/28040.

Heynen, N., McCarthy, J., Prudham, S., and Robbins, P. (eds.) (2007), *Neoliberal Environments: False Promises and Unnatural Consequences*. Abingdon, UK: Routledge.

Hickel, J. (2020), *A Response to McAfee: No, the "Environmental Kuznets Curve" Won't Save Us*, https://www.jasonhickel.org/blog/2020/10/9/response-to-mcafee.

Himmelweit, S. (2017), *Changing Norms of Social Reproduction in an Age of Austerity*. Unpublished manuscript.

Hirschman, A. (1958), *The Strategy of Economic Development*. New Haven, CT: Yale University Press.

Hoexter, M.F. (2014), *Governments Can and Must Lead Climate Action via Public Investment*, Global Institute for Sustainable Prosperity, November. http://www.global-isp.org/wp-content/uploads/PN-103.pdf.

Hoffmann, U. (2011), *Some Reflections on Climate Change, Green Growth Illusions and Development Space*, United Nations Conference on Trade and Development, December, https://unctad.org/en/PublicationsLibrary/osgdp2011d5_en.pdf.

Hoffmann, U. (2015), *Can Green Growth Really Work and What Are the True (Socio-) Economics of Climate Change?*United Nations Conference on Trade and Development, July, https://unctad.org/en/PublicationsLibrary/osgdp2015d4_en.pdf.

Hudson, M. (2010), "From Marx to Goldman Sachs: The Fictions of Fictitious Capital, and the Financialization of Industry," *Critique* 38 (3), pp. 419–444.

Hujo, K. (2012), *Mineral Rents and the Financing of Social Policy*. London: Palgrave.

IER (2016), *Exploring the Dangers of the Keep It In the Ground Campaign*, Institute for Energy Research, April 26, https://www.instituteforenergyresearch.org/fossil-fuels/coal/dangers-keep-ground-campaign/.

IMF (2005), *The Macroeconomics of Managing Increased Aid Inflows: Experiences of Low-Income Countries and Policy Implications*. Washington, DC: IMF.

IMF (2019), *Fiscal Monitor: How to Mitigate Climate Change*, https://www.imf.org/en/Publications/FM/Issues/2019/10/16/Fiscal-Monitor-October-2019-How-to-Mitigate-Climate-Change-47027.

IPCC Working Group I (1995), "Summary for Policymakers: The Science of Climate Change," in B. McKibben (ed.), *The Global Warming Reader: A Century of Writing about Climate Change*. London: Penguin.

IPCC Working Group I (2018), "Global Warming of 1.5oC," https://www.ipcc.ch/site/assets/uploads/sites/2/2019/06/SR15_Full_Report_High_Res.pdf.

ITF (2015), *The Carbon Footprint of Global Trade*, https://www.itf-oecd.org/carbon-footprint-global-trade.

Jakob, M. and Hilaire, J. (2015), "Unburnable Fossil-Fuel Reserves," *Nature* 517, pp. 150–152.

Jalilian, H. and Kirkpatrick, C. (2005), "Does Financial Development Contribute to Poverty Reduction?," *Journal of Development Studies* 41 (4), pp. 636–656.

Johansson, A. (2016), *Public Finance, Economic Growth and Inequality: A Survey of the Evidence*, Working Paper #1346, Organisation for Economic Co-Operation and Development, November. https://ideas.repec.org/p/oec/ecoaaa/1346-en.html.

Johnson, O.W., Gerber, V., and Muhoza, C. (2018), "Gender, Culture and Energy Transitions in Rural Africa," *Energy Research & Social Science* 49, pp. 169–179.

Jomo K.S. and B. Fine (eds.) (2006), *The New Development Economics: After the Washington Consensus.* Delhi: Tulika.

Jorgenson, A.K. (2014), "Economic Development and the Carbon Intensity of Human Well-Being," *Nature Climate Change* 4, pp. 186–189.

Joslin, A. (2019), "Translating Water Fund Payments for Ecosystem Services in the Ecuadorian Andes," *Development and Change* 51 (1), pp. 94–116.

Joya, O. (2015), "Growth and Volatility in Resource-Rich Countries: Does Diversification Help?" *Structural Change and Economic Dynamics* 35, pp. 38–55.

Kakwani, N. (2001), *Pro-Poor Growth and Policies.* Manila: Asian Development Bank.

Kakwani, N. (2002), *Pro-Poor Growth and Policies.* UNDP Asia-Pacific Regional Programme on the Macroeconomics of Poverty Reduction, www.undp.org.

Kakwani, N. and Pernia, E.M. (2000), "What Is Pro-Poor Growth?" *Asian Development Review* 18, pp. 1–16.

Kallis, G., Kerschner, C., and Martinez-Alier, J. (2012), "The Economics of Degrowth," *Ecological Economics* 84, pp. 172–180.

Kaplinsky, R. and Farooki, M. (2012), *Promoting Industrial Diversification in Resource Intensive Economies*, United Nations Industrial Development Organization, https://bit.ly/3uplOZw.

Kartha, S., Kemp-Benedict, E., Ghosh, E., Nazareth, A., and Gore, T. (2020), *The Carbon Inequality Era: Joint Research Report, SEI and Oxfam*, https://www.sei.org/publications/the-carbon-inequality-era/.

Keen, S. (2017), "Trade and the Gains from Diversity," *Globalizations* 14 (6), pp. 803–809.

Kelkar, G. and Nathan, D. (2005), *Gender Relations and the Energy Transition in Rural Asia*, United Nations Development Fund for Women, South Asia Regional Office, http://citeseerx.ist.psu.edu/viewdoc/download?doi=10.1.1.856.7578&rep=rep1&type=pdf.

Kemp, R. and Never, B. (2017), "Green Transition, Industrial Policy, and Economic Development," *Oxford Review of Economic Policy* 33 (1), pp. 66–84.

Khor, M. (2011), *Risks and Uses of the Green Economy Concept in the Context of Sustainable Development, Poverty and Equity*, South Centre, July, https://citeseerx.ist.psu.edu/viewdoc/download?doi=10.1.1.357.7714&rep=rep1&type=pdf.

Khor, M., Montes, M.F., Williams, M., and Yu III, V.P. (2017), *Promoting Sustainable Development by Addressing the Impacts of Climate Change*

Response Measures on Developing Countries, Research Paper 81, South Centre, https://www.southcentre.int/research-paper-81-november-2017/.

Kidd, S. (2017), "Citizenship or Charity: The Two Paradigms of Social Protection," *Pathways' Perspectives on Social Policy in International Development* 25, http://www.developmentpathways.co.uk/wp-content/uploads/2017/11/Citizenship-or-Charity-PP25-1-1.pdf.

KinderMorgan (2020), *The Need for Fossil Fuels*, October, http://www2.kindermorgan.com/getAttachment/4c844b12-9ecd-4948-a44f-ee3ebef02173/White_Fossil_Fuels.pdf.

Kuznets, S. (1955), "Economic Growth and Income Inequality," *American Economic Review* 45 (1), pp. 1–28.

Lahn, G. and Bradley, S. (2016), *Left Stranded? Extractives-Led Growth in a Carbon-Constrained World*, Research Paper. London: The Royal Institute of International Affairs.

Langley, P. and Mellor, M. (2002), "'Economy,' Sustainability and Sites of Transformative Space," *New Political Economy* 7 (1), pp. 49–65.

Lavinas, L. (2017), *The Brazilian Paradox: The Takeover of Social Policy by Financialization*. London: Palgrave.

Lavoie, M. (2014), "Financialization, Neo-liberalism, and Securitization," *Journal of Post Keynesian Economics* 35 (2), pp. 215–233.

Lawson, M., Chan, M., Rhodes, F. . . ., and Gowland, R. (2019), *Public Good or Private Wealth?*, Oxfam International, January. https://www.oxfam.org/en/research/public-good-or-private-wealth.

Lazear, E.P. (2000), "Economic Imperialism," *Quarterly Journal of Economics* 115 (1), pp. 99–146.

Le Goff, M. and Singh, R.J. (2013), *Does Trade Reduce Poverty? A View from Africa*, Policy Research Working Paper 6327, World Bank, January, https://openknowledge.worldbank.org/handle/10986/12165.

Le Quéré, C., Jackon, R., Jones, M. . . ., and Peters, G. (2020), "Temporary Reduction in Daily Global CO2 Emissions during the COVID-19 Forced Confinement," *Nature Climate Change* 10, pp. 647–653.

Lederman, D. and Maloney, W.F. (2012), *Does What You Export Matter?* Washington, DC: World Bank.

Leibovici, F. and Crews, J. (2018) *Trade Liberalization and Economic Development*, Economic Synopses 13, Federal Reserve Bank of St. Louis. https://research.stlouisfed.org/publications/economic-synopses/2018/04/20/trade-liberalization-and-economic-development.

Leubolt, B., Fischer, K., and Saha, D. (2013), *Targeting and Universalism: Complementary or Competing Paradigms in Social Policy? Insights from Brazil, India and South Africa*. Unpublished manuscript.

Lieu, J., Sorman, A.H., Johnson, O.W., Virla, L.D., and Resurreccion, B.P. (2020), "Three Sides to Every Story: Gender Perspectives in Energy Transition Pathways in Canada, Kenya and Spain," *Energy Research & Social Science* 68, doi:10.1016/j.erss.2020.101550.

Lim, Mah-Hui and Lim, J. (2012), *Asian Initiatives at Monetary and Financial Integration: A Critical Review*. Unpublished manuscript.

List, F. (1885 [1841]), *The National System of Political Economy*. London: Longmans, Green and Co.

Listo, R. (2018), "Gender Myths in Energy Poverty Literature: A Critical Discourse Analysis," *Energy Research & Social Science* 38, pp. 9–18.

Lohmann, L. (2009), "Climate as Investment," *Development and Change* 40 (6), pp. 1063–1083.

Loureiro, P. and Saad-Filho, A. (2019), "The Limits of Pragmatism: The Rise and Fall of the Brazilian Workers' Party (2002–2016)," *Latin American Perspectives* 46 (1), pp. 66–84.

Lukauskas, A., Stern, R.M., and Zanini, G. (2013), *Handbook of Trade Policy for Development*. Oxford: Oxford University Press.

Lysandrou, P. (2018), "The Causal Primacy of Global Inequality in the Financial Crisis," *Theory and Struggle* 119 (1), pp. 24–34.

MacEwan, A. (2003), "*Debt and Democracy: Can Heavily Indebted Countries Pursue Democratic Economic Programs?*" Paper presented at the symposium "Common Defense against Neoliberalism," Istanbul.

Mahroum, S. and Al-Saleh, Y. (2016), *Economic Diversification in Natural Resource Rich Economies*. New York: Routledge.

Manganelli, S. and Popov, A. (2010), *Finance and Diversification*, Working Paper #1259, European Central Bank, October. https://www.ecb.europa.eu/pub/pdf/scpwps/ecbwp1259.pdf.

Manganelli, S. and Popov, A. (2015), "Financial Development, Sectoral Reallocation, and Volatility: International Evidence," *Journal of International Economics* 96 (2), pp. 323–337.

Manley, D., Cust, J., and Cecchinato, G. (2017), *Stranded Nations? The Climate Policy Implications for Fossil Fuel-Rich Developing Countries*, Policy Paper 34, Oxford Centre for the Analysis of the Resource-Rich Economies, https://papers.ssrn.com/sol3/papers.cfm?abstract_id=3264765.

Marois, T. (2021), *Public Banks: Decarbonisation, Definancialisation and Democratisation*. Cambridge: Cambridge University Press.

McCulloch, N. and Baulch, B. (1999), *Assessing the Poverty Bias of Growth: Methodology and an Application to Andhra Pradesh and Uttar Pradesh*. Working Paper #98, Institute of Development Studies, https://www.ids.ac.uk/publications/assessing-the-poverty-bias-of-growth-methodology-and-an-application-to-andhra-pradesh-and-uttar-pradesh/.

McElwee, P., Huber, B., and Vân, N.T.H. (2019), "Hybrid Outcomes of Payments for Ecosystem Services Policies in Vietnam: Between Theory and Practice," *Development and Change* 51 (1), pp. 253–280.

McGlade, C. and Ekins, P. (2015), "The Geographical Distribution of Fossil Fuels Unused When Limiting Global Warming to 2°C," *Nature* 517, pp. 187–203.

McKibben, B. (ed.) (2011a), *The Global Warming Reader: A Century of Writing about Climate Change*. London: Penguin.

McKibben, B. (2011b), "Introduction," in *The Global Warming Reader: A Century of Writing about Climate Change*, pp. 9–15. London: Penguin.

McKibben, B. (2016), "A World at War," *The New Republic*, August 15. https://newrepublic.com/article/135684/declare-war-climate-change-mobilize-wwii.

McKinley, T. (ed.) (2001), "Introduction," in *Macroeconomic Policy, Growth and Poverty Reduction*, pp. 1–15. London: Palgrave.

McKinley, T. (2003), *The Macroeconomics of Poverty Reduction: Initial Findings of the UNDP Asia-Pacific Regional Programme*. New York: UNDP.

McKinley, T. (2004), *MDG-Based PRSPs Need More Ambitious Economic Policies*. Unpublished manuscript.

McKinley, T. (2009), *Revisiting the Dynamics of Growth, Inequality and Poverty Reduction*, SOAS Discussion Paper, Centre for Development Policy and Research, September 25, http://citeseerx.ist.psu.edu/viewdoc/download?doi=10.1.1.472.9855&rep=rep1&type=pdf.McKinnon, H., Muttitt, G. and Sproul, E. (2017), *The Sky's Limit: Why Norway Should Lead the Way in a Managed Decline of Oil and Gas Extraction*. Washington, DC: Oil Change International.

Mechling, G., Miller, S., and Konecny, R. (2017), "Do Piketty and Saez Misstate Income Inequality?" *Review of Political Economy* 29 (1), pp. 30–46.

Mikesell, R.F. (1997), "Explaining the Resource Curse, with Special Reference to Mineral Exporting Countries," *Resources Policy* 23 (4), pp. 191–199.

Milanovic, B. (2016), *Global Inequality: A New Approach for the Age of Globalization*. Cambridge, MA: Belknap Press.

Millward-Hopkins, J., Steinberger, J.K., Rao, N.D., and Oswald, Y. (2020), "Providing Decent Living with Minimum Energy: A Global Scenario," *Global Environmental Change* 65, https://doi.org/10.1016/j.gloenvcha.2020.102168.

Morrissey, J. (2016), *Who Should Sell the Last of the Fossil Fuels: Stranded Assets, Equity and Climate Change*, Oxfam, May 9, https://politicsofpoverty.oxfamamerica.org/2016/05/who-should-sell-the-last-of-the-fossil-fuels-stranded-assets-equity-and-climate-change/.

Muradian, R., Arsel, M., Pellegrini, L., … and Aguilar, B. (2013), "Payments for Ecosystem Services and the Fatal Attraction of Win-Win Solutions," *Conservation Letters* 6 (4), pp. 274–279.

Muttitt, G. (2018), *Off Track: How the International Energy Agency Guides Energy Decisions Towards Fossil Fuel Dependence and Climate Change*, Oil Change International and Institute for Energy Economics and Financial Analysis, April, http://priceofoil.org/content/uploads/2018/04/OFF-TRACK-the-IEA-Climate-Change.pdf.

Naschold, F. (2004), "Growth, Distribution, and Poverty Reduction: LDCs Are Falling Further Behind," in A. Shorrocks and R. van der Hoeven (eds.), *Growth, Inequality, and Poverty: Prospects for Pro-Poor Economic Development*, pp. 107–124. Oxford: Oxford University Press.

Nayyar, D. (2015). "Globalization and Democracy," *Brazilian Journal of Political Economy* 35 (140), pp. 388–402.

Nelson, S.H., Bremer, L.L., Meza Prado, K., and Brauman, K.A. (2019), "The Political Life of Natural Infrastructure: Water Funds and Alternative Histories of Payments for Ecosystem Services in Valle del Cauca, Colombia," *Development and Change* 51 (1), pp. 26–50.

Nersisyan, Y. and Randall Wray, L. (2019), *How to Pay for the Green New Deal*, Working Paper #931, Levy Economics Institute, May. http://www.levyinstitute.org/publications/how-to-pay-for-the-green-new-deal.

Newell, P. and Simms, A. (2019), "Towards a Fossil Fuel Non-Proliferation Treaty," *Climate Policy* 20 (8), pp. 1043–1054.

Nuroglu, E. and Kunst, R.M. (2018), "Kuznets and Environmental Kuznets Curves for Developing Countries," in M.A. Yülek (ed.), *Industrial Policy and Sustainable Growth*, pp. 1–14. Singapore: Springer.

ODI (2013), *The Geography of Poverty, Disasters and Climate Extremes in 2030*, https://www.odi.org/sites/odi.org.uk/files/odi-assets/publications-opinion-files/8634.pdf.

OECD (2011), *Economic Diversification in Africa*. Paris: OECD.

OECD (2015), *In It Together: Why Less Inequality Benefits All*, https://www.oecd.org/social/in-it-together-why-less-inequality-benefits-all-9789264235120-en.htm.

Onaran, O. and Guschanski, A. (2018), *The Causes of Falling Wage Share*, Greenwich Political Economy Research Centre, https://gala.gre.ac.uk/id/eprint/19373/7/19373%20ONARAN_The_Causes_of_Falling_Wage_Share_2018.pdf/.

Oparaocha, S. and Dutta, S. (2011), "Gender and Energy for Sustainable Development," *Energy Research & Social Science* 3 (4), pp. 265–271.

Osmani, S. R. (2001), *Growth Strategies and Poverty Reduction. Asia and Pacific Forum on Poverty: Reforming Policies and Institutions for Poverty Reduction*. Manila: Asian Development Bank.

Ossowski, R. and Halland, H. (2019), "Key Aspects of Fiscal Management in Resource-Rich Countries," in A. Huurdeman and A. Rozhkova (eds.), *Balancing Petroleum Policy*, pp. 101–149. Washington, DC: World Bank.

Ostry, J.D., Berg, A., and Kothari, S. (2018), *Growth-Equity Trade-Offs in Structural Reforms*, International Monetary Fund, January 5, https://www.imf.org/en/Publications/WP/Issues/2018/01/05/Growth-Equity-Trade-offs-in-Structural-Reforms-45540.

Ouedraogo, N.S. (2020), "Transition Pathways for North Africa to Meets Its (Intended) Nationally Determined Contributions under the Paris Agreement," *Climate Policy* 20 (1), pp. 71–94.

Pachauri, S. and Rao, N.D. (2013), "Gender Impacts and Determinants of Energy Poverty: Are We Asking the Right Questions?," *Current Opinion in Environmental Sustainability* 5 (2), pp. 205–215.

Page, J. (2008), *Rowing against the Current: The Diversification Challenges in Africa's Resource Rich Economies*, Working Paper #68, UNU-WIDER, June, https://www.wider.unu.edu/publication/rowing-against-current.

Palanivel, T. (2003), *Report of the Regional Workshop on Macroeconomics of Poverty Reduction*. New York: UNDP.

Palma, G. (1998), "Three and a Half Cycles of 'Mania, Panic and [Asymmetric] Crash': East Asia and Latin America Compared," *Cambridge Journal of Economics* 22 (6), pp. 789–808.

Panayotakis, C. (2007), "Working More, Selling More, Consuming More: Capitalism's 'Third Contradiction'," in L. Panitch and C. Leys (eds.), *Coming to Terms with Nature*, pp. 254–272. Monmouth, NJ: Monthly Review Press.

Panitch, L. and Gindin, S. (2012), *The Making of Global Capitalism: The Political Economy of American Empire.* London: Verso.

Pasha, H.A. and Palanivel, T. (2004), *Pro-Poor Growth and Policies: The Asian Experience.* New York: UNDP.

Perkins, P.E. (2007), "Feminist Ecological Economics and Sustainability," *Journal of Bioeconomics* 9, pp. 227–244.

Perrons, D. (2015), "Gendering the Inequality Debate," *Gender and Development* 23 (2), pp. 207–222.

Peszko, G., Golub, A., Marjis, C., … and Midgley, A. (2020), *Diversification and Cooperation in a Decarbonizing World.* Washington, DC: World Bank Group.

Pickett, K. and Wilkinson, R. (2010), *The Spirit Level: Why Equality Is Better for Everyone.* London: Penguin.

Piketty, T. (2014), *Capital in the Twenty-First Century.* Cambridge, MA: Harvard University Press.

Prebisch, R. (1950), *The Economic Development of Latin America and Its Principal Problems.* New York: ECLA. http://archivo.cepal.org/pdfs/cdPrebisch/002.pdf.

Rajagopal, Z.V. (2018), "International Trade Policies and Development," in *Business Dynamics in North America*, pp. 183–216. London: Palgrave Macmillan.

Rao, J.M. (2002), *The Possibility of Pro-Poor Development: Distribution, Growth and Policy Interactions*, Unpublished manuscript.

Raval, A., Sheppard, D. and Khalaf, R. (2020), "BP Warns of Oil Demand Peak by Early 2020s," *Financial Times*, 14 September, https://www.ft.com/content/7a6d5cb2-0e7e-4ea5-8662-5ac75c4c0694.

Raworth, K., Wykes, S., and Bass, S. (2014), *Securing Social Justice in Green Economies*, International Institute for Environment and Development, October, https://pubs.iied.org/16578IIED/.

Reinert, E. (2008), *How Rich Countries Got Rich … and Why Poor Countries Stay Poor.* New York: PublicAffairs.

Reinert, E., Ghosh, J., and Kattel, R. (eds.) (2018), *Handbook of Alternative Theories of Economic Development.* Cheltenham, UK: Edward Elgar.

Rezai, A. and Stagl, S. (2016), "Ecological Macroeconomics: Introduction and Review," *Ecological Economics* 121, pp. 181–185.

Ricardo, D. (2014 [1821]), *On the Principles of Political Economy and Taxation*, Scotts Valley, CA: CreateSpace Independent Publishing Platform.

Ritchie, H. (2017), *How Much Will It Cost to Mitigate Climate Change?* Our World in Data, May 27, https://ourworldindata.org/how-much-will-it-cost-to-mitigate-climate-change.

Robbins, P. (2020), "Is Less More ... Or Is More Less? Scaling the Political Ecologies of the Future," *Political Geography* 76, doi:10.1016/j.polgeo.2019.04.010.

Ross, M. (2008), "Oil, Islam, and Women," *American Political Science Review* 102 (1), pp. 107–123.

Ross, M. (2017), *What Do We Know about Economic Diversification in Oil-Producing Countries?*University of California, Los Angeles, January 24, https://papers.ssrn.com/sol3/papers.cfm?abstract_id=3048585.

Rosser, A. (2006), *The Political Economy of the Resource Curse*, Working Paper 268, Brighton, UK: Institute of Development Studies.

Ryan, S.E. (2014), "Rethinking Gender and Identity in Energy Studies," *Energy Research & Social Science* 1, pp. 96–105f.

Saad-Filho, A. (2007), "There Is Life beyond the Washington Consensus: An Introduction to Pro-Poor Macroeconomic Policies," *Review of Political Economy* 19 (4), pp. 513–537.

Saad-Filho, A. (2011), "Growth, Poverty and Inequality: Policies and Debates from the (Post-)Washington Consensus to Inclusive Growth," *Indian Journal of Human Development* 5 (2), pp. 321–344.

Saad-Filho, A. (2015), "Social Policy for Neoliberalism: The Bolsa Família Programme in Brazil," *Development and Change* 46 (6), pp. 1227–1252.

Saad-Filho, A. (2017), "Neoliberalism," in D.M. Brennan, D. Kristjanson-Gural, C. Mulder, and E. Olsen (eds.), *The Routledge Handbook of Marxian Economics*, pp. 245–254. London: Routledge.

Saad-Filho, A. (2018), "Monetary Policy and Neoliberalism," in D. Cahill, M. Cooper, and M. *Konings* (eds.), *SAGE Handbook of Neoliberalism*, pp. 335–346. London: SAGE.

Saad-Filho, A. (2019), *Value and Crisis: Essays on Labour, Money and Contemporary Capitalism*. Leiden: Brill.

Saad-Filho, A. (2021), *Growth and Change in Neoliberal Capitalism: Essays in the Political Economy of Late Development*. Leiden: Brill.

Saad-Filho, A. and Johnston, D.J. (eds.) (2005), *Neoliberalism: A Critical Reader*. London: Pluto Press.

Saad-Filho, A. and Weeks, J. (2013), "Curses, Diseases, and Other Resource Confusions," *Third World Quarterly* 34 (1), pp. 1–21.

Sachs, J.D. and Warner, A.M. (1995), *Natural Resource Abundance and Economic Growth*, Working Paper No. 5398, National Bureau of Economic Research, December, https://www.nber.org/papers/w5398.

Saia, A., Andrews, D., and Albrizio, S. (2015), *Productivity Spillovers from the Global Frontier and Public Policy: Industry-Level Evidence*, Working Paper #1238, Organisation for Economic Co-Operation and Development, June. https://www.oecd-ilibrary.org/economics/spillovers-from-the-global-productivity-frontier-and-public-policy_5js03hkvxhmr-en.

Sander, K. and Cranford, M. (2010), *Financing Environmental Services in Developing Countries*, World Bank, December 1, http://documents.worldbank.org/curated/en/100131468330884916/Financing-environmental-services-in-developing-countries.

Sapinski, J.P., Buck, H.J., and Malm, A. (eds.) (2020), *Has It Come to This? The Promises and Perils of Geoengineering on the Brink*. New Brunswick, NJ: Rutgers University Press.

Scales, I. (2014), "Paying for Nature: What Every Conservationist Should Know about Political Economy," *Oryx* 49 (2), pp. 226–231.

Schwerhoff, G., Edenhofer, O., and Fleurbaey, M. (2020), "Taxation of Economic Rents," *Journal of Economic Surveys* 34 (2), pp. 398–423.

Seguino, S. (2019), "Engendering Macroeconomic Theory and Policy," *Feminist Economics 26* (2), pp. 27–61.

SEI, IISD, ODI, E3G, and UNEP (2020), *The Production Gap Report: 2020 Special Report*, http://productiongap.org/2020report.

Sekar, S., Lundin, K., Tucker, C., ... and Aguilar, J. (2019a), *Policy Approaches to Climate Change in Mineral Rich Countries, Background Paper for Building Resilience: A Green Growth Framework for Mobilizing Mining Investment*. Washington, DC: World Bank.

Sekar, S., Lundin, K., Tucker, C., Figueiredo, J., Tordo, S., and Aguilar, J. (2019b), *Methodology and Value Chain Analysis: Background Paper for Building Resilience: A Green Growth Framework for Mobilizing Mining Investment*. Washington, DC: World Bank.

Sen, A., Fattouh, B., Moerenhout, T., and Luciani, G. (2019), "Introduction," *Forum* 118, 1–4, https://www.bakerinstitute.org/media/files/files/35891108/oef-118-krane.pdf.

Serfati, C. (2003), "La dominación del capital financiero: ¿qué consecuencias?" in F. Chesnais and D. Plihon (eds.), *Las trampas de las finanzas mundiale*, pp. 59–72. Madrid: Akal.

Shaikh, A. (1979–1980), "Foreign Trade and the Law of Value," *Science & Society* 43 (4), pp. 281–302 and 44 (1) 1980, pp. 27–57.

Shapiro-Garza, E. (2019), "An Alternative Theorization of Payments for Ecosystem Services from Mexico," *Development and Change*, 51 (1), pp.196–223.

Siddiqui, K. (2015), "Trade Liberalization and Economic Development," *International Journal of Political Economy* 44 (3), pp. 228–247.

Siebert, J. (2020), "The Greening of Uneven and Combined Development: IR, Capitalism and the Global Ecological Crisis," *Cambridge Review of International Affairs*, doi:10.1080/09557571.2020.1823943.

Sinclair-Desgagné, B. (2013), *Greening Global Value Chains*, Working Paper #6613, World Bank, September, https://papers.ssrn.com/sol3/papers.cfm?abstract_id=2328452.

Singer, H. (1950), "The Distribution of Gains between Investing and Borrowing Countries," *American Economic Review* 40 (2), pp. 473–485.

Slemrod, J. (1995), "What Do Cross-Country Studies Teach about Government Involvement, Prosperity and Economic Growth?" *Brookings Papers on Economic Activity* 2, pp. 373–430.

Solati, F. (2017), *Women, Work, and Patriarchy in the Middle East and North Africa*. London: Palgrave.

Solow, R.M. (1956), "A Contribution to the Theory of Economic Growth," *Quarterly Journal of Economics* 70 (1), pp. 65–94.

Storm, S. (2009), "Capitalism and Climate Change: Can the Invisible Hand Adjust the Natural Thermostat?" *Development and Change* 40 (6), pp. 1011–1038.

Storm, S. (2011), "WDR 2010: The World Bank's Micawberish Agenda for Development in a Climate-Constrained World," *Development and Change* 42 (1), pp. 399–418.

Storm, S. (2017), "The Political Economy of Industrialization," *Development and Change*, doi:10.1111/dech.12281.

Studart, R. (2005), "The State, the Markets and Development Financing," *Cepal Review* 85, pp. 19–32.

Szirmai, A. (2012), "Industrialisation as an Engine of Growth in Developing Countries, 1950–2005," *Structural Change and Economic Dynamics* 23 (4), pp. 406–420.

Taylor, L., Rezai, A., and Foley, D. (2016), "An Integrated Approach to Climate Change, Income Distribution, Employment, and Economic Growth," *Ecological Economics* 121, pp. 196–205.

Terrones, M. and Catão, L. (2001), *Fiscal Deficits and Inflation*, International Monetary Fund, May. https://www.elibrary.imf.org/view/IMF001/02476-978145 1849592/02476-9781451849592/02476-9781451849592_A001.xml?language= en&print.

Thompson, A. (2020), "Neighborhood Wealth Dramatically Impacts Home Greenhouse Gas Emissions," *Scientific American*, 1 November, https://www.scientificamerican.com/article/neighborhood-wealth-dramatically-impacts-home-greenhouse-gas-emissions/.

Tomasi, J. (2015), "Market Democracy and Meaningful Work: A Reply to Critics," *Res Publica* 21, pp. 443–460.

Turner, A. (2020a), "The Costs of Tackling Climate Change Keep on Falling," *Financial Times*, 11 December, https://www.ft.com/content/33bb3714-93cf-4af5-9897-e5bf3b013cb7.

Turner, A. (2020b), *Are Rich Countries Shirking Their Carbon Responsibilities?* World Economic Forum and Project Syndicate, 24 February, https://www.weforum.org/agenda/2020/02/rich-world-responsibility-carbon-footprint-climate- change/.

UNCTAD (2002), *Economic Development in Africa Report: From Adjustment to Poverty Reduction: What is New?* Geneva: UNCTAD.

UNCTAD (2012), *Trade and Development Report*. Geneva: UNCTAD.

UNCTAD (2019), *State of Commodity Dependence*. Geneva: UNCTAD.

UNDESA (2013), *World Economic and Social Survey*, New York: UNDESA.

UNDP (2002), *The Role of Economic Policies in Poverty Reduction*. New York: UNDP.

UNDP (2005), *The Wealth of the Poor: Managing Ecosystems to Fight Poverty*. New York: UNDP.

UNDP (2013), *Humanity Divided: Confronting Inequality in Developing Countries,*https://www.undp.org/content/undp/en/home/librarypage/poverty-reduction/ humanity-divided–confronting-inequality-in-developing-countries.html.

UNFCCC (2005), *The Concept of Economic Diversification in the Context of Response Measures,* https://unfccc.int/sites/default/files/resource/Technical% 20paper_Economic%20diversification.pdf.

UNFCCC (2007), *Review of the Experience of International Funds, Multilateral Financial Institutions and Other Sources of Funding Relevant to the Current and Future Investment and Financial Needs of Developing Countries,* https://digitallibrary.un.org/record/614170?ln=ar.

UNFCCC (2016), *Just Transition of the Workforce, and the Creation of Decent Work and Quality Jobs,* https://unfccc.int/sites/default/files/resource/Just% 20transition.pdf.

UNFCCC (2018a), *UN Climate Change Annual Report,* https://unfccc.int/sites/ default/files/resource/UN-Climate-Change-Annual-Report-2018.pdf.

UNFCCC (2018b), *Entry Points for Integrating Gender Considerations into UNFCCC Workstreams,* https://unfccc.int/sites/default/files/resource/TP% 20overview_Gender%20Dialogue.pdf.

UNIDO (2015), *Global Green Growth Report,* Vol. 1, https://www.unido.org/ sites/default/files/2015-05/GLOBAL_GREEN_GROWTH_REPORT_vol1_ final_0.pdf.

UNIDO and GGGI (2015), *Global Green Growth: Clean Energy Industrial Investments and Expanding Job Opportunities*Volume II, https://gggi.org/report/ global-green-growth-clean-energy-industrial-investments-and-expanding-job-opportunities/.

UNRISD (2012), *Social Dimensions of the Green Economy,* https://sustainabledevelopment.un.org/index.php?page=view&type=400&nr=479&menu=1515.

UNRISD (2017), *Transformative Policies for Sustainable Development: What Does It Take?* https://www.unrisd.org/unrisd/website/document.nsf/(httpPublications)/6456C5E375AEE153C1258176003FBF05?OpenDocument.

UNRISD (2018), *Mapping Just Transition(s) to a Low-Carbon World,* https:// www.unrisd.org/80256B3C005BCCF9/(httpPublications)/9B3F4F10301092C7 C12583530035C2A5.

UN Women (2015), *Progress of the World's Women, 2015–2016,* https://progress.unwomen.org/en/2015/.

USAID (1998), *Handbook of Democracy and Governance Program Indicators.* Washington, DC: USAID.

Utting, P. (ed.) (2015), *Revisiting Sustainable Development.* Geneva: UNRISD.

Vandemoortele, J. (2004), *Can the MDGs Foster a New Partnership for Pro-Poor Policies?*Unpublished manuscript.

Van Waeyenberge, E. (2006), "From Washington to Post-Washington Consensus: Illusions of Development," in K.S. Jomo and B. Fine (eds.), *The New Development Economics after the Washington Consensus,* pp. 21–45. London: Zed Books.

Vercelli, A. (2017), *Crisis and Sustainability: The Delusion of Free Markets.* London: Palgrave.

Versteeg, R.J. (2008), "Capital Controls and Economic Growth: How Controls on Inflows and Outflows are Different," Maastricht University, https://www.researchgate.net/publication/228177387_Capital_Controls_and_Economic_-Growth_How_Controls_on_Inflows_and_Outflows_are_Different.

Vieira, C. (2000), *Are Fiscal Deficits Inflationary? Evidence for the EU*, Department of Economics, Loughborough University, April. https://www.researchgate.net/publication/2638323_Are_Fiscal_deficits_inflationary_Evidence_for_the_EU.

Wachtel, H.M. (2000), "Tobin and Other Global Taxes," *Review of International Political Economy* 7 (2), pp. 335–352.

Warner, A.M. (2014), *Public Investment as an Engine of Growth*, Working Paper #14/148, International Monetary Fund, August. https://www.imf.org/external/pubs/ft/wp/2014/wp14148.pdf.

WDR (2010), *World Development Report: Development and Climate Change*. Washington, DC: World Bank.

WEF (2015), *What Is the Link between Carbon Emissions and Poverty?*, https://www.weforum.org/agenda/2015/12/what-is-the-link-between-carbon-emissions-and-poverty/.

Weingast, B. (2015), *Capitalism, Democracy, and Countermajoritarian Institutions*, Department of Political Science, Stanford University, August 4, https://papers.ssrn.com/sol3/papers.cfm?abstract_id=2639793.

Weller, C. E. and Hersh, A. (2004), "The Long and Short of It: Global Liberalization and the Incomes of the Poor," *Journal of Post Keynesian Economics* 26 (3), pp. 471–504.

Wiedman, T., Lenzen, M., Keysser, L., and Steinberger, J.K. (2020), "Scientists' Warning on Affluence," *Nature Communications* 11 (3107), https://www.nature.com/articles/s41467-020-16941-y.

Wiig, A. and Kolstad, I. (2012), "If Diversification Is Good, Why Don't Countries Diversify More? The Political Economy of Diversification in Resource-Rich Countries," *Energy Policy* 40, pp. 196–203.

Wiig, A. and Kolstad, I. (2018), "Diversification and Democracy," *International Political Science Review* 39 (4), pp. 551–569.

Winters, L.A. (2002), "Trade Policies for Poverty Alleviation," in B. Hoekman, A. Mattoo, and P. English (eds.), *Development, Trade, and the WTO*. Washington, DC: World Bank.

Woertz, E. (2014). "Mining Strategies in the Middle East and North Africa," *Third World Quarterly* 35 (6), pp. 939–957.

World Bank (2009), *What Is Inclusive Growth?* http://siteresources.worldbank.org/INTDEBTDEPT/Resources/468980-1218567884549/WhatIsInclusive-Growth20081230.pdf.

World Bank (2017), *The Growing Role of Minerals and Metals for a Low Carbon Future*. Washington, DC: World Bank.

World Bank (2018), *Reinvigorating Growth in Resource-Rich Sub-Saharan Africa*, http://documents.worldbank.org/curated/en/617451536237967588/Reinvigorating-Growth-in-Resource-Rich-Sub-Saharan-Africa.

Yülek, M.A. (2018), "Industrial Policy and Sustainable Development," in M.A. Yülek (ed.), *Industrial Policy and Sustainable Growth*, pp. 1–24. Singapore: Springer.

Zen, F. (2011), *Economic Diversification: The Case of Indonesia*, Working Paper, Revenue Watch Institute, https://resourcegovernance.org/sites/default/files/RWI_Econ_Diversification_Indonesia.pdf.

Zysman, J. (1983), *Governments, Markets and Growth*. Ithaca, NY: Cornell University Press.

Index

126   *Index*

132   *Index*

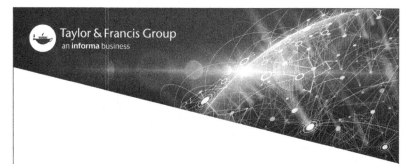

Printed in the United States
by Baker & Taylor Publisher Services